A CELEBRATION OF MUTTS

The Underdog

by Julia Szabo

for Daisy

Copyright © 2005 by Julia Szabo

All rights reserved. No portion of this book may be reproduced—mechanically, electronically, or by any other means, including photocopying—without written permission of the publisher. Published simultaneously in Canada by Thomas Allen & Son Limited.

Cover design by Lisa Hollander
Book design by Lisa Hollander and Denise Sommer

Library of Congress Cataloging-in-Publication Data is available.

ISBN-10: 0-7611-3348-8
ISBN-13: 978-0-7611-3348-3

Workman books are available at special discounts when purchased in bulk for premiums and sales promotions as well as for fund-raising or educational use. Special editions or book excerpts can also be created to specification. For details, contact the Special Sales Director at the address below.

Workman Publishing Company, Inc.
708 Broadway
New York, NY 10003-9555
www.workman.com

Printed in the United States of America
First printing October 2005

10 9 8 7 6 5 4 3 2 1

The Underdog

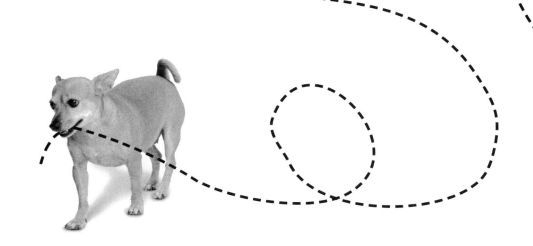

Tiki is my beloved chow-rottweiler mix. He is my mutt muse. Once he was abandoned then overlooked at an animal shelter. Today he is a mutt-about-town whose good looks always turns heads. This book is a celebration of Tiki and his underdog brethren.

Okay, you're a dog person. But are you a mutt person? You are if you're a trendsetter, an individualist, an iconoclast, a creative, free-spirited type. And you are in good company. Meet other Mutt Mavens throughout history and learn why the unbreed is the one to have.

Money can't buy mutt love, so avoid pet stores and head straight to your local animal shelter. Here is all you need to know about the adoption process.

What happens when a dalmatian meets a pit bull? When Chihuahua meets

Lab? When shepherd meets terrier? A genealogy unlike any other—complete with photos of glorious canine "cocktails."

CHAPTER 4
Sound Mutt, Sound Body
• 115 •

If health is wealth, mutts are rich indeed. Mixed breeds are healthier and live longer than purebreds. Here's how to maximize hybrid vigor and overcome and prevent illness.

CHAPTER 5
Oh, Behave!
• 145 •

Think of mutts as certified preowned pets. Many are perfectly well behaved, with no issues. Others may require a refresher course in good behavior. This is it.

CHAPTER 6
La Dolce Vita
• 187 •

Make room on the sofa. No dog moves from the mean streets to easy street with as much panache as a mutt. Decor, travel plans, toys, wardrobe— a guide to the good life for mutts and their people.

APPENDIX
The Ulti-Mutt Resource Guide
• 235 •

All the goodies and services featured throughout the book. Plus surprises.

Isaac Mizrahi
and Harry

Foreword

I never met a Mutt I didn't like,

and let me tell you, there are plenty of humans I can't
bear--which is why I see things now from a dog's perspective,
not a human's. It's a kind of transformation that has
occurred in my life, a crazy giving over to my true
nature, the nature I never knew I even possessed before
I adopted Harry. My life needed to be derailed, messed
up slightly; I needed to get in touch with my inner
mutt. I like to think Harry and I get along because we're
opposites. He's not in the least bit ironic, nor does he
have a sleep disorder. Or a weight problem. And he's not
a postmodernist. We complement each other in ways that no
humans possibly could. Before Harry, I was merely human.
I'm all dog now, an honorary member of the K9 race. All
those years before Harry, I had to seek out reasons and
opportunities to be nonhuman. Then the K9 thing happened
to me, and once it did, I embraced it. I actually wrote
this foreword in dog and had it translated; it's the
language I write best in. I don't miss being human at all.
Being human is highly overrated anyway.

--Isaac Mizrahi

Carrying a Torch for Tiki

I am looking at a dog named Tiki. I love looking at Tiki; I look at him a lot, and I'm not the only one. Even on the streets of Manhattan, which fairly crawl with gorgeous creatures, Tiki gets a lot of looks because, well, he's a looker. He's a parlor-size lion with a glossy raven coat, blueberry-stained tongue, and the deepest, roundest brown eyes that ever gazed into mine. Passersby often stop to scratch his head and say, "What a nice dog!" or "What breed is that?" The best part is, Tiki's not a breed at all; he's a mutt.

What is a mutt? Strictly speaking, a mutt is the offspring of two different breeds of dog. If your purebred beagle accidentally tangles with a neighbor's golden retriever and puppies are born, the pups in that litter are mutts. Sometimes those pups are kept and loved as family pets; often, they are not, and they end up at an animal shelter. In a broader sense, mutts include any dog whose existence was unplanned, or who was ever, at any time in his life, unwanted or deemed unsightly, flawed, abused, handicapped, abandoned, or a stray. Mutts are underdogs.

Left: Two views of Tiki the Choweiler, by Martha Szabo.

To look at my Tiki today, you'd be hard-pressed to call him an underdog. His chow-rottweiler-maybe-even-some-Newfoundland coat is glossy and unique. His personality is effervescent. He is relaxed—pampered beyond belief and generally enjoying the good life. But five years ago, he was marked for euthanasia at an animal shelter in upstate New York, one month after his original family had moved house and left him behind. Back then he was called Tinky. (I'm not sure what was more disgraceful: his first family's failing to appreciate him, or their saddling him with such an unworthy handle.) Names can be changed easily enough. But for years, the notion of *mutt* carried a stigma. No more. Mutts have come out of the shadows of history and into the limelight.

Why have mutts suddenly found favor after centuries of scorn? There are many reasons: Mutts are generally healthier than purebreds. It feels good to rescue an animal from certain doom. And the smart set—Hollywood stars, fashion designers, and other trendsetters —has declared that mutts are the new "it" dogs. Why get something off the rack when you can have something that's one of a kind? Would Tiki get as much attention if he were just a chow, or a rottie, or a Newfy? Of course not. He'd look like every other chow, rottie, or Newfy on the block. He certainly wouldn't be such

"Do not follow where the path may lead. Go instead where there is no path, and leave a trail."

--RALPH WALDO EMERSON

a friendly guy if he were all chow. Purebred chows tend to be reserved and aloof, in keeping with the purpose for which they were bred: guard duty. But when chows are mixed with other types of dog, that *en garde* attitude is softened; they become outgoing and even cuddly.

Purebreds are predictable, and in some cases they attract people who are status hounds, social climbers, and wannabes. In the world of the purebred, the holy grail is conformation. And conformation is, frankly, boring. Mutts, on the other hand, are always a delightful surprise. People who fancy mutts tend to be iconoclasts. They don't live or die for the snob appeal of

Why get something off the rack when you

owning a papered, pedigreed dog. They have no problem being "owned by" a dog with mysterious markings, mysterious habits, and a mysterious past.

This book, like the nonconformist dogs it celebrates, is a hybrid, combining mutt history, culture, and appreciation with nuts-and-bolts information on caring for these unique, lovable pets. Its pages incorporate advice on subjects as varied as how to adopt a mutt, how to have fun identifying your mutt's mystery origins, and resources for out-of-the-ordinary ways to pay tribute to your one-of-a-kind dog.

Why take my word on this subject? Because, I'm proud to say, I share my life with five mutts, three of them rescued from animal shelters, two from the street. Because I'm obsessive about showing them the best time I can, and because, as a writer focusing on animal issues, I'm constantly on the lookout for goods and services that will improve my mutts' quality of life. Animals have no voice, so I've dedicated my career to speaking out on their behalf in the media, in my weekly "Pets" column for the *New York Post* and my monthly "You & Your Pet" column for *Country Living* magazine. My inspiration is the hardworking title character of E. B. White's *Charlotte's Web*. Early on, I was impressed that the arachnid heroine of that beautiful story deployed her writing skills to help others. I've been lucky to make my living reporting on and researching what I love best: animals. In *The Underdog,* I'm sharing my love of mutts with you in the hopes that you and your underdog share a lifetime of joy.

Whether you're a confirmed mutt lover already or think you might have what it takes to become one, I hope you'll find something in these pages to inform and surprise you. The brilliant dogs you'll meet in this book are a rare breed indeed: one in a million *and* a dime a dozen, yours for the taking at your local animal shelter (and sometimes on a sidewalk or highway near you). Let this book help you connect with the best friend and most loving family member you will ever know.

can have something that's one of a kind?

Welcome to the Tribe

CHAPTER 1

There are two kinds of people in this world:

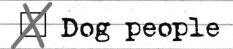 **Dog people**

☐ **and everyone else**

You know dog people right away. They tend to be warm, bighearted, generous. They are curious. They appreciate close relationships. It takes commitment to care for a dog, and they've got it. Pets of all species, of course, require love and attention, but dogs even more so. They need food, shelter, and all the basics of care that any domestic animal needs, but dogs also need you. They require companionship in a way that other animals don't. They are pack animals who recognize the safety in numbers, even if the number is only two. They want to be with us as much as we do with them. Little wonder we love them so much and become so devoted to them.

Dog Person vs. Mutt Person

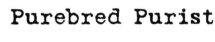

Once you realize you are a dog person, you need to find the pet that's right for you. And here dog people split into two camps—sometimes without even realizing it, sometimes intentionally, and sometimes with a foot in each camp:

☐ **Purebred Purist**
☐ **Mutt Maven**

A Purebred Purist is drawn to a certain breed. She may have a long history of having that breed. She may have a friend with one. The breed may have struck her fancy on television or in film. Or she may be looking for certain traits that the breed displays. An athletic person may want a black Lab who would enjoy jogging with him. A sedentary, elderly person might want a bulldog or dachshund, whose exercise requirements are less demanding. An allergy sufferer might choose a breed with soft hair like a poodle or shih tzu. Someone interested in security looks for a guarding breed like a rottweiler or a German shepherd.

For some Purebred Purists, a snob factor is involved. They want a dog with papers. Even if they themselves don't have a pedigree—let's face it, most

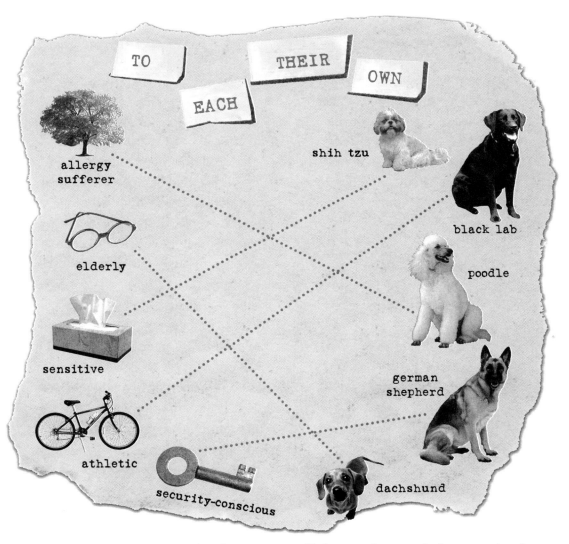

TO EACH THEIR OWN

allergy sufferer

shih tzu

black lab

elderly

poodle

sensitive

german shepherd

athletic

security-conscious

dachshund

Americans don't—their purebred pet will. And the dog will be able to compete in dog shows, a beloved pastime of status hounds.

Sometimes fashion dictates the desire for a specific breed. The British royal fam-ily has set dog trends for centuries, from King Charles II and the small spaniel named for him to Queen Elizabeth II, who has kept corgis since her childhood and has kept the breed in the spotlight. Celebrities have made other breeds the dog du jour: stripper Gypsy Rose Lee boosted the profile of Chinese cresteds when she quipped that the dog is dressed just like her at the climax of her act. FDR had Scottish terriers, creating a craze for not only the dog, but also for collectibles (doorstops, stuffed animals, and the like) created in the breed's

image. Moose, the dog who played Eddie on the television sitcom *Frasier,* caused a run on Jack Russell terriers, while the live-action remake of the Disney film *101 Dalmatians* inspired thousands of people to buy spotted puppies.

The rise of the unbreed

Mutts, on the other hand, are the plain brown wrapper of dogdom. They are the generic brand, a no-name animal, the unbreed. At one time, they were dirty vermin, unwanted pests. Dogcatchers in the nineteenth century were paid a bounty to dispose of them like so much trash. But one era's trash is another's treasure.

Call it enlightenment, call it radical chic—nowadays, mutts are hot dogs. Why?

Every mutt is one of a kind, and in these days of mass-produced merchandise, of branding run rampant, the mutt's uniqueness is a priceless commodity. Mutts are not perfect, and that's their appeal. Mutt Mavens relate to their imperfections and find their irregularities adorable. You won't find a snaggletooth in a well-bred dog. You won't see asymmetrical ears. You won't have the charm of crazy-quilt patches and spots. Each mutt's quirks are entirely her own.

call it recycling, call it radical

Mutts have no pretensions. They are survivors who get by on their wits and pluck. They have no trophies to brandish, no name to trade on. There's no nepotism here. Chalk up their successes to merit, spunk, and hard work.

Most mutts are better behaved than their purebred peers. They are healthier, having not been inbred. They tend to live longer. Most play well with others—both canine and human. They are smart and easy to train. They seem to appreciate all that you do for them. They are ideal for families.

Rescuing a mutt is a form of recycling. It's a socially responsible, noble thing to do. It feels good to give someone a second chance. Mutts breed good vibes.

snaggletooth

NOBODY'S PERFECT

crazy-quilt patches

asymmetrical ears

spots

chic, the mutt is the "it" dog.

A Muttley Crew

Some interesting profiles emerge when you look at the people behind the mutts. In broad strokes, Mutt Mavens are creative, self-made, independent people. They are quirky and fun. Many believe in doing the right thing, but at the same time, they try not to take themselves too seriously. There are several archetypes of mutt people that you see all the time. If you are a mutt person, you might fall into one of these categories. Or you might not—you might be as unique as your dog.

Hyphenate

Just as there is the Lab-chow-shepherd-terrier, there is the director-actor-producer-author-decorator-filmmaker. These are multitalented multitaskers; people who wear many hats. Famous hyphenates include actor-producers Kevin Bacon, Sandra Bullock, Julia Roberts; primatologist-conservationist Jane Goodall; personality-guru Dr. Phil; and comedienne-producer Lucille Ball.

Lucille Ball

Julia Roberts

Dr. Phil

Political Animal

John F. Kennedy

Lyndon Johnson

These people adopt a mutt because it's the right thing to do. They have the courage of their convictions and strong beliefs. Some of them work in government—many rising to the top levels—others work in the local food co-op. This crosses the boundaries of mere party affiliation—call it bipawtisan, if you will. JFK and Lyndon Johnson both had mutts. (See page 13 for more political animals.)

Troubadour

These are the wanderers. Most are musical; all are artistic. They appreciate freedom. Don't fence them in. Sheryl Crow, Morrissey, Alanis Morissette, Nellie McKay, and Moby are just a few musicians who are Mutt Mavens.

k. d. lang

Anthony Kiedis with Muddy

Paul McCartney

Pupwardly Mobile

David Duchovny & Téa Leoni

Matthew Broderick & Sarah Jessica Parker

Phoebe Cates & Kevin Kline

You get married. You buy a house. You have a child. Then you have another. Time to get a dog. Why not a mutt? Russell and Kimora Lee Simmons, athletes Laird Hamilton and Gabrielle Reece, and Kevin Kline and Phoebe Cates all have mutts.

Stray Pride

Many gays and lesbians are as out loud and proud about their pets as they are about their own lives. They're mixed. They're fixed. Get used to it.

Elton John

Ellen DeGeneres

Harvey Fierstein

The Young and the Beautiful

Christian Bale

Hilary Swank

Secure in their own talents, looks, and burgeoning incomes, these boldface names don't require an attention-getting purebred. Think Natalie Portman, Orlando Bloom, Renée Zellweger, Jake Gyllenhaal, Zach Braff, and Mary-Kate Olsen.

Literary Lions

Authors who are known Mutt Mavens include Maxine Kumin, A. M. Homes, Mark Doty, Paul Auster, Siri Hustvedt, Ann Patchett, Kien Nguyen, Melissa Pierson, and Luc Sante.

Paul Auster

Mark Doty

Mutt's the GOOD Word?

by Martha Barnette

The word *mutt* derives from a much older term, one inspired by an entirely different animal. *Mutt* comes from *muttonhead,* a contemptuous word that recalls the proverbial stupidity of sheep. Since the early 1800s, *muttonhead* has been used to mean "a dull-witted, foolish person."

> *Mutt comes from muttonhead, a contemptuous word that recalls the proverbial stupidity of sheep.*

Over time, however, speakers of English sheared the final two syllables from *muttonhead* and applied the shortened form, *mutt,* to anyone considered similarly dopey or stupid. By the early 1900s, the meaning of the word *mutt* had expanded to include dogs as well. (In 1906, for example, one American writer, Helen Green, voiced a complaint that will be familiar to many mutt lovers: "A fellow can't leave nothin' on his bed without that mutt chawin' it up!") Today the word *mutt* most often refers to a mixed-breed dog, but its secondary definition remains "a stupid person or simpleton."

If terms for *mutt* in other languages are any indication, mixed-breed dogs fare no better in many other places. The Spanish word for mutt, *chucho,* sounds like what it means: "scram!" or "shoo!" In Denmark and Lithuania, the words for mutt translate as "peasant's dog"—a dog as poor as its owners, in other words. In the Netherlands, a mutt is a *vuilnisbakkenras,* or "garbage-bin dog." And in Brazil, a mutt is commonly called a *vira-lata*—a term that literally means "it turns the can" and conjures the poignant image of a starving pup scrounging for food in an alley.

In some countries, mutts go by names that are even more derogatory. In Korea, where there's a long tradition of eating dogs—one that historically included hanging or beating the animal to soften its flesh before slaughter—a mutt is called a *ddong kae*, or literally "shit dog." A similar idea informs a common word for *mutt* in Greece, where most people live amicably with legions of large dogs roaming cities like Athens, but dark reports still circulate about mass poisonings of strays. In Greece, the word for *mutt* is *kopritis*, which derives from the Greek for "shit."

Leave it to those romantic Germans, though, to come up with a somewhat warmer word for *mutt: Promenadenmischung.* This Teutonic mouthful derives from two words meaning "promenade mixture"—an expression, some say, that suggests the dog was the result of an amorous encounter between two pooches who first locked eyes (or rumps and noses, as the case may be) while out for an afternoon stroll.

THE BAHA-MUTT

In the Bahamas, strays are affectionately called "pot-cakes" because of the diligent way they lick the cookware put out for them until it's clean of scraps. Animal lover Frances Hayward of the Humane Society of Grand Bahama has taken several starving pot-cakes under her wing, including a mutt named Amigo (pictured). Schooled in obedience and agility by animal trainer Bill Grimmer, Amigo is now the poster boy in the "I'm a Bahamian too" public-service campaign Hayward designed to promote kindness to Caribbean strays.

Amigo with Frances Hayward

MUTT'S IN A NAME?

We've come a long way from the time when mutt was a put-down. Many people are proud to incorporate the M-word in their names. Star skateboarder Rodney Mullen's nickname is "The Mutt," and noted record producer Robert John Lange, who has produced albums for Shania Twain and AC/DC, among others, is renowned in the entertainment industry as "Mutt" Lange. Mariah Carey's purebred Jack Russell terrier is called Jack, short for Jackson P. Muttley. But for those who still feel the M-word carries a stigma, the Arnell Memorial Humane Society in Amery, Wisconsin, calls eligible female dogs "Society Girls."

A MUTT BY ANOTHER NAME

France - batard

Italy - bastardo

Queen's English - mongrel

Japan - zattshu

Hungary - keverek

Sweden - byracka

American Kennel Club (AKC) Speak - cur

Norway - bastard

Puerto Rico - sato

One Nation Under Dog

American history abounds with hounds of uncertain parentage. No less an American president than Abraham Lincoln was devoted to his mutt, Fido. The dog was a constant companion who would carry parcels for Lincoln and wait patiently outside Billy the Barber's in Springfield, Illinois, while Lincoln got his hair cut. As if we didn't already have enough reason to admire this particular American leader, Lincoln's treatment of his mutt and his sensitivity to the dog's needs speak volumes about his upstanding character.

When he was elected president in 1860, Lincoln decided not to take five-year-old Fido to Washington because he feared the stress of the long train trip might kill him. (Fido was afraid of noises like church bells and cannons.) So Lincoln decided to leave the dog in the care of his neighbor, John Roll, a carpenter who had helped remodel the Lincolns' house. Lincoln instructed the family never to tie Fido up in the backyard or scold him for tracking mud into the house on his paws, and he made sure Fido would always be allowed in the dining room at mealtimes. He even gave Roll the horsehair sofa on which Fido had grown accustomed to reclining.

After living the good life the president had secured for him, Fido passed away less than a year after Lincoln was assassinated, in 1865. Because Fido didn't make it to the White House, he and his kind remained under the radar for many more years.

Several other presidents have had mutts. The Grant family kept many animals, but mutt Rosie, unlike the family's other dogs, was cared for by the coachman, Albert. Just as well. Jesse Grant, the president's son, indicated in his memoirs that the family did not have a good track record of keeping dogs alive for very long. The twentieth president, James Garfield, had a mixed-breed named Veto, while the twenty-third president, Benjamin Harrison, had several mutts, including one named Dash.

Families with lots of children tend to find themselves with lots of dogs. When Theodore Roosevelt and his wife, Edith, moved with their six children into the White House in the early twentieth century, a menagerie of pets followed. One of the dogs was a mongrel named Tip, whom Mrs. Roosevelt particularly liked. Mrs. Roosevelt cringed when staff members referred to Tip as a mutt, but she had a sense of humor to accompany her Victorian distaste for unpleasant words. After Tip ran away, Mrs. Roosevelt adopted another mixed-breed dog. This one she straight-out named Mutt. President Roosevelt's favorite dog was a

Teddy Roosevelt's favorite dog was a stray, and probably also a mutt.

stray, and probably also a mutt. He found Skip on a trip to the Grand Canyon. A feisty, playful little dog, Skip accompanied the president on hunting trips in the West. When the dog couldn't keep up the pace, the president gave Skip a ride with him in the saddle.

In 1957, the entire world was captivated by a four-legged Russian cosmonaut, the first animal to go into orbit—and, as it happens, a mutt. On November 3, 1957, the Soviet Union launched the world's second artificial space satellite, *Sputnik 2,* from the Baikonur Cosmodrome. Harnessed into the capsule was a three-year-old Siberian husky mix named Laika (Russian for "barker"), one of the many female strays picked up on the Moscow streets and trained for space travel. Nicknamed "Muttnik" by the American press, Laika was hooked

Politicians and pundits love a shaggy-dog story, and some love a shaggy dog, too. These Washington insiders and commentators all embrace the mutt, proving that you don't have to be a yellow-dog Democrat to love a mutt.

JFK Jr. *The dashing heir to Camelot was secure in his own pedigree, so he chose a mutt named Friday as his running (and cycling and rollerblading) mate. Friday, who usually traveled with the Kennedys, was not on the doomed Piper Saratoga that took his master's life.*

Al Gore. *Daisy, a shaggy gray-and-white mixed-breed, saw the Gores through the nail-biting 2000 presidential campaign. Found as a stray by the Gore children, Daisy was initially called Inspector Turnip—until Tipper discovered the pup's endearing habit of dozing in flower beds.*

Jon Stewart. *The host of* The Daily Show *has a mutt. And how appropriate. As mutts blur the lines between breeds, so Stewart has artfully combined hard news and humor, putting a fresh spin on the "evening news." His colleague Lewis Black also loves mutts, as do writer-comedienne-radio personalities Lizz Winstead and Janeane Garofalo.*

Senator John Kerry. *Although his family has a purebred German shepherd, the senator rescued a mutt in Vietnam and told us all about it—many times—during his 2004 run for president.*

Representative Marsha Blackburn. *Blackburn has two mutts, Indy and Betty. "We always go to our local animal shelter and adopt mixed-breed dogs," says the Tennessee congresswoman.*

up to a life-support system, her vital signs monitored by electrodes to see how a living organism would react to spaceflight. She reacted admirably, despite a harness that left her almost no room to move. Her capsule was rigged with food, water, even padded walls, but it was not designed for recovery.

Laika the mutt aboard *Sputnik 2*.

Mutts in space

Laika was doomed, sacrificed by the very scientists who trained her. Her life-support batteries ran down about a week after launch, and she died of asphyxiation. *Sputnik 2* fell into the atmosphere in April 1958; the capsule and its passenger were incinerated. Forty years after her flight, Laika was remembered in a monument to honor fallen cosmonauts at Star City outside Moscow, as well as on a plaque at the Moscow research center where she was trained for space flight. In 1998, one of the scientists on the early Soviet space program, Oleg Gazenko, said at a Moscow news conference, "The more time passes, the more I'm sorry about it. We shouldn't

have done it. . . . We did not learn enough from this mission to justify the death of the dog." In August 1960, two more female mutts, Strelka (Russian for "little arrow") and Belka ("squirrel") orbited Earth eighteen times aboard *Sputnik 5*. They were recovered safely, and Strelka later gave birth to six puppies. One, Pushinka ("fluffy"), was given as a gift to President John F. Kennedy, who accepted despite the CIA's concern that the dog was bugged. This being in the time of pre–spay-neuter awareness, Pushinka quickly mated with the Kennedys' Irish terrier Charlie, and JFK called her litter of puppies (what else?) "pupniks."

Yuki and Johnson howled

Party animals

No president doted on his mutt as much as Lyndon Johnson did on Yuki. The Johnsons had been beagle people until daughter Luci brought home a stray she'd found wandering around a gas station in Texas. Johnson and Yuki became inseparable. She accompanied him everywhere, from cabinet meetings to the swimming pool. Mrs. Johnson drew the line when Johnson tried to include her in portraits of Luci's wedding. Yuki and Johnson howled duets together in the Oval Office to the delight of the American public, who lapped up photos of the sing-alongs.

The Iran hostage crisis and the gasoline shortage weren't the only low points of the Carter administration. Young Amy Carter had been given a mutt, Grits, by one of her teachers, but the dog never really settled into the family. Carter himself had grown up with a beloved mutt, Bozo, but Grits proved more of a challenge and the family returned him to Amy's teacher. On a more positive note, Carter's vice president, Walter Mondale, adored his beagle mix, Digger. Initally adopted by the Mondales' daughter Eleanor, the lucky mutt lived in the vice president's house as well as in the ambassador's residence in Tokyo, where Mondale was later posted. After her death, at age seventeen, Digger was buried in Japan, and the Mondales named their weekend home in Minnesota "Diggerwood."

duets together in the Oval Office

Who's top dog now!

E Pluribus Unum

America chose a bald eagle as a symbol of the nation, but we might have been truer to ourselves if we had chosen a mutt, who is one dog out of many.

The Melting Pot. The mutt, like so many Americans, is the result of cross-breeding. He's a canine melting pot, reveling in the diversity of his roots rather than slavishly following a standard. The more in the mix, the terrier, er, merrier.

Manifest Destiny. She may have been a wanderer, a stray. Many mutts adhere to a creed of manifest destiny as they roam the land in search of greener pastures and a farther frontier. The mutt has an independent spirit.

Meritocracy. Unlike his purebred counterparts, the North American shelter hound doesn't ride on his own or his ancestors' good looks. He gets ahead on merit alone. He's no *Mayflower* descendant; he's a maverick. He's a dog after Horatio Alger's heart. He started with nothing, and got by on up-by-your-bootstraps pluck.

Local Hero. The mutt next door is the dog next door: a sweet, lovable, populist pet. He's not perfect, but he's always trying to make good. Peering out from behind shelter bars in hometowns across the country, he is hopeful for a brighter tomorrow and will do anything for a chance at self-improvement. He's an all-American original—just give him a shot, and you'll see.

And the Winner Is...

People are starting to celebrate mutts by awarding them prizes. (Seems unfair that only purebreds have been winning all the ribbons thus far.)

In May 2004, TV's *Live with Regis and Kelly* hosted the first annual "Mutt America Pageant," and it's now an annual tradition. The contest's rules declare emphatically "No purebreds allowed!" and canine contestants were flown in from all over the country for this entertaining, weeklong spoof of Miss America, including four-legged talent competitions and makeovers (but thankfully no swimsuits). The top dog won a $5,000 PETsMART gift certificate and an appearance with Regis Philbin and Kelly Ripa on the cover of *Modern Dog*, the glossy lifestyle magazine for urban dogs. Not surprisingly, two of the show's producers,

Cindy MacDonald and Lori Schulweis, are proud mutt people.

Every December in New York, a group called Tails in Need sponsors the online Great American Mutt Contest, inviting Mutt Mavens to submit their dog's photograph and a brief write-up explaining why he or she is the Great American Mutt. After deliberations by a panel of celebrity judges (full disclosure: I was one of them), Tails in Need announced the 2004 winner: a mutt named Toby, who was born with no eyes. Toby amazed his adoptive family with his ability to get around and learn basic obedience (with the help of hot dogs). Upon first meeting Toby, most people don't even realize that he can't see.

TV producer Lori Schulweis's mutt Molly, who helped inspire the creation of the "Mutt America Pageant" on *Live with Regis and Kelly*.

Where the Mutts Are

the hows and whys of adoption

Ca•nis /kayn-us/ n. the chief and type genus of the family Canidae that includes the domestic dog, the wolves and jackals, and sometimes in older classifications the foxes.

DOG
General view of the Superficial muscles of neck, chest and shoulder.

Let There Be Mutt

How did the mutt come to be? It's actually a better question to ask how purebreds came to be, because mutts actually came first. At some fateful point in prehistory, a wolf decided to cozy up to a human, marking the beginning of a beautiful friendship. Eventually, the descendants of that wolf evolved into *Canis lupus familiaris,* the domesticated species we know as dog.

In the Beginning . . .

The primordial canine was wolflike, resembling a rougher, less-refined version of those lupine-looking breeds, the husky and German shepherd. Over time, taking cues from the different climates inhabited by his new two-legged pack leader, the dog adapted himself for survival. Prehistoric paintings show canines resembling a cross between a wolf and a gazelle: a fleet-footed creature accompanying his nomadic humans in the hunt.

The human need to impose order spurred the categorization and naming of different dog breeds. As early as the 1200s, canines with specific physical characteristics and talents—like hunting, herding, and guarding—began to be codified. This was important to the people who used dogs in their work. If a dog was good at herding sheep, she would be bred with another herding dog to ensure that the shepherd was working with the kind of dog best suited to the job. Eventually, many of the groups of dogs and breeds we know today became recognizable.

> Every purebred began as the result of a mix.

There was the terrier, who hunted rats; the chow chow, who stood guard duty; the border collie, who herded the flock. Maintaining groups of dogs and specific breeds was vital to human survival; without the dogs, granaries would be overrun with rats, property would be looted by thieves, flocks would be diminished or dispersed.

Every purebred began as the result of a mix. For example, bulldog and terrier were combined to create the Staffordshire bull terrier, a dog with a knack for ratting, who was also

strong enough to pull heavy carts. The pointer's lineage is foxhound, greyhound, and bloodhound. The English setter was produced by crossing Spanish pointer, water spaniel, and springer spaniel; the Gordon setter came about through mixing the bloodhound and the collie, among others. The strong, fearless bullmastiff is, as his name suggests, a cross between a bulldog and a mastiff; the bull terrier and Boston terrier were created by mating a bulldog to the now-extinct English white terrier (also a forebear of the Jack Russell) and the English terrier, respectively. And then there are the numerous dogs bred to assist in the hunt for specific quarry, from birds (retrievers) to rabbits (spaniels) to badgers (dachshunds) to lions (Rhodesian ridgebacks). These are all legitimate purebreds now, but it's not a stretch to say that they are just highly sophisticated mixes.

He looks like a huge, hairy mutt, but the Leonberger is a purebred originally created by combining the Saint Bernard, Newfoundland, and Greater Swiss mountain dog.

Some European dog breeds tend to resemble mutts more than purebreds. The Leonberger is a fine example: The "lion dog" is the result of careful cross-breeding in the 1840s by Heinrich Essig, mayor of the German town Leonberg. The breed is a hybrid of Saint Bernard, Newfoundland, and Greater Swiss mountain dog—and he looks like the biggest, cutest mutt you've ever seen. The Berger de Picard (or Picardy shepherd), a French herding breed, looks like a wiry-bearded terrier mix and resembles a mutt enough to have been cast as the lead in the 2005 movie version of the shaggy-mutt tale *Because of Winn-Dixie*.

The codification of breeds was made official in 1884 with the formation of the American Kennel Club (AKC), whose motto is "For the love of the purebred dog." The AKC maintains a purebred registry, sanctions all dog show events in the country (including the prestigious Westminster Kennel Club Dog Show, see page 24), and has continuously published its monthly magazine, the *AKC Gazette*, since 1889. If a breed is not recognized by the AKC—even if it's an ancient breed recognized in, say, Europe—the dog cannot compete in American dog shows.

You may feel good about your pedigreed purebred, but realize that when you reach way back to the animal's past, he's not all that different from a mutt.

The purebred dog

A purebred is the result of careful, selective breeding by people for whom canine genetics may be a hobby, a profession, or an obsession. Purebred dogs, the fruits of breeders' labors, are the supermodels of the canine world who compete for ribbons at dog shows, which are essentially canine beauty pageants. The three most prestigious purebred shows in dogdom are the Westminster Kennel Club Dog Show, held every February in New York City; the National Dog Show, held every November in Philadelphia; and the AKC/Eukanuba National Championship, held every January in a different location. At these shows, all of which are televised, judges examine each dog for "conformation" or strict adherence to a breed standard. Many of the physical traits that endear mutts to mutt lovers—an undershot bite,

MUTT MYSTERY SOLVED

Mutt people can't help wondering what happened to the rest of their beloved's littermates. Most of us never find out, but Barbara and Patricia Dury actually did. In 1991, the sisters went to check out a litter of ten prenamed nine-week-old mixed-breed pups—"Benji" types—at the Peace Plantation, a sanctuary in New York's Delaware County. They adopted one and named her Molly, but they never got Molly's siblings off their minds, especially one named Tessa. One day eight years later, while shopping for vegetables at a farmers' market, Barbara happened to notice a car pull up and a woman step out with a fluffy white mutt. "Pat said to me, that looks a lot like Molly—why don't you go over and see where she got the dog?" It was Tessa.

As it turned out, Tessa had wound up at a different Delaware County animal shelter, the Delhi Animal Shelter, about six months earlier, because her original guardian had thrown her out of the house. Later, that "guardian" thought better of her misdeed and called the shelter demanding the dog back (which is how they learned her name was Tessa). The shelter sued to keep Tessa and won—and Tessa was adopted in short order by Linda Stutz, the woman Barbara and Patricia met at the farmers' market. The Durys are now friends with Linda and her husband, Ron, who summer in the Catskills and winter in Florida; as for the mutt sisters, wary of each other at first, they now entertain each other during visits.

Mutt sisters Molly and Tessa: littermates reunited through sheer coincidence. Portraits by Martha Szabo.

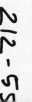

irregular ears, a nonconformist attitude—automatically disqualify "defective" purebreds from even entertaining thoughts of entering a dog show.

The show of shows is the Westminster Kennel Club Dog Show. Westminster held its first dog show in 1877 at a New York arena called Gilmore's Garden, the forerunner of Madison Square Garden, which today hosts Westminster every February for two straight days, the second Monday and Tuesday of the month. Despite the dubious physical fitness of some of the participants, Westminster is a sporting event—in fact, it's the country's second-oldest continuously held sporting event after the Kentucky Derby. No canine of mixed, random breeding will ever be awarded a purple ribbon at Westminster, which is open only to purebred champions (dogs who have won a certain number of ribbons at other dog shows elsewhere in the country). However, one mutt *is* welcome: Gromit, the animated costar of Dreamworks's popular "Wallace and Gromit" franchise, whose mixed parentage was no obstacle to his hosting the streaming video coverage of the 2005 Westminster show on the WKC's Web site.

Unlike shelter mutts, who are spayed or neutered, Westminster contenders must be "intact"; dog breeding, after all, is a lucrative business (dogs can cost $4,000 and up), so breeders mate champions with each other and sell the pups. Westminster contenders also have two names: a champion name and a call name. For example, the 2004 Best in Show winner was a Newfoundland named Ch. Darbydale's All Rise Pouch Cove. His mouthful of a name incorporates that of his owners' breeding kennel, Darbydale. A handler would quickly lose a dog's attention using such a long name every time she wanted him to sit and stay. That's why all Westminster champs also have a call name that's significantly shorter, if not monosyllabic. In 2004, everyone in America was on a call-name basis with "Josh" the Newfoundland

ka-ching!

because, the day after, the Westminster winner traditionally makes the rounds of television shows, from *Good Morning America* to *The Charlie Rose Show*.

A purebred trots around a dog show ring.

MUTTS ACROSS THE POND

The English counterpart to Westminster is Crufts, which started in 1891 and is now in its 115th year (it takes place every March in Birmingham, England). But Mutt Mavens in the U.K. have their own prestigious event that draws nationwide attention, the competition where no pedigreed dog need apply: Scruffts. Sponsored by the U.K. pet-food giant PAL and now in its fifth year, the aptly named Scruffts is a celebration of mongrels, or crossbreeds (as British mutts are called), with regional heats culminating in the announcement, every November in London, of Britain's Ultimate Crossbreed. Classes (that's categories to us Yanks) include Most Handsome Crossbreed Dog, Prettiest Crossbreed Bitch, Child's Best Friend, and The Crossbreed the Judge Would Most Like to Take Home.

FOR PITS' SAKE

Besides being the subject of much controversy and the victim of misunderstanding and intolerance, perceived as more demon than dog, the pit bull, short for American pit bull terrier, is not a recognized breed; the AKC recognizes only the American Staffordshire terrier and Staffordshire bull terrier. Yet all three—pit bull, American Staffordshire, and Staffordshire bull—are hybrids of bulldog and terrier, and they share so many physical characteristics they are almost indistinguishable from one another. This book embraces pit bulls as mutts.

A hybrid of bulldog and terrier, and an animal too often maligned by the media, the pit bull is a bona fide underdog. Portraits by Dirk Westphal.

NOTE BOOK

Gotta Getta Dog

When you decide to get a dog, you have three choices:

☐ ~~Go to a pet store~~ **PICK THIS ONE**

☐ Go to a breeder

☐ Go to a shelter ◄

The **first option is not an option.** Never buy a dog from a pet store. Pet stores procure their stock from "puppy mills"—unethical breeders who mistreat their animals and do not breed carefully. The dogs are often sickly and many times have serious congenital conditions. They are abused from the moment they are born until the time they are discarded—when they can no longer breed. Reputable breeders are a good option if you are certain of the breed you want. They raise their dogs in humane conditions and breed carefully. Reputable breeders are found through word of mouth or through the AKC. The last—and in my opinion, best—option is a shelter.

Gimme shelter

Animal shelters are treasure troves of untapped canine potential, packed to the rafters—quite literally—with underdogs. You never know who you'll find there, and you'll never see the same dog twice. Don't worry about being overwhelmed: The shelter staff will work hard to help you find your ideal underdog canine mate.

Animal shelters are not-for-profit corporations that offer refuge to unwanted dogs and cats (and sometimes other species as well), making pets available for adoption to the public. Most shelters have a small reception area that opens into kennels, where dogs are kept in individual cages. In rural and suburban areas, those cages have vertically sliding doors big enough for the dogs to let themselves out into a chain-link-fenced pen where they can relieve themselves. In overcrowded urban shelters, the dogs are walked once or twice a day; the rest of the day is spent in cages stacked two high. Urban shelters have one or at most two bigger cages for oversize breeds.

Shelters may sound like awful places. Being in a cage all day with the looming threat of being destroyed by lethal injection is nobody's idea of fun, least of all a dog's, but it's not the worst fate an animal could suffer. At least the dog isn't vulnerable to predators or speeding automobiles, and he has a chance of being adopted into a new home. Space is limited; in addition to owner-surrendered dogs,

shelters are a refuge for strays: dogs found wandering the roads and streets until they are picked up by animal-control officers, dogs whose guardians died with no next of kin, dogs who one way or another became lost, or stolen, then lost.

Shelter staffers are made up of workers and teams of volunteers. In between promoting adoptions and doing kennel duty, patient shelter staffers try to take the time to train and socialize the dogs in their care. Often, local professional trainers will donate their time to shelters for basic training to help make dogs more adoptable, starting them on the path to becoming perfectly eligible pets. Sometimes, local grooming professionals will also donate their time at shelters, giving makeovers to scruffy mutts to help them look their best.

A TOOTH FOR A TOOTH

In 2004, newswires were alight with the man-bites-dog tale of a man in Pensacola, Florida, who tried to shoot a litter of mutt puppies and wound up getting shot himself. As he juggled his .38-caliber revolver at the wiggling creatures, one of the dogs put his paw on the trigger, and the gun fired at the man's arm. The man took himself to the hospital, where he was treated, then charged with felony animal cruelty. The surviving puppies—Trigger (the marksmutt), Remington, Winchester, and Colt—were hailed as heroes and put up for adoption.

Shelter Dogs

Here's a who's who of the types of underdogs you might meet in your local shelter.

Abandoned Purebreds. Purebred dogs, just like mutts, sometimes end up homeless. They get lost, are abandoned, or are surrendered by families who decide for one reason or another that they can't handle a dog anymore. Some of these dogs find their way to animal shelters. Usually, when a purebred dog ends up at a crowded animal shelter, the shelter will call the local chapter of the breed rescue group, and someone from that organization will assume care and work to find the dog a new home.

Flawed Purebreds. Certain purebreds might be said to have more in common with mutts than with their pedigreed peers. These are purebreds who fall short of their breed standards in one or more crucial ways. Some Rhodesian ridgebacks are born without the distinctive "zipper" of against-the-grain hair running down their backs. German shepherds may be born white. Purebred dogs with flaws are considered worthless in the eyes of Purebred Purists. Luckily, devotees of these misfits

take meeee!

I'll be nice and clean.

you guys are making fools of yourselves.

what about me?

dedicate themselves to rescuing and re-homing "impurebreds" with recessive genes. These dog lovers want to make sure no representative of their beloved breed becomes an animal shelter statistic. The advantage for purebred fanciers who feel guilty about spending big bucks on a dog while so many languish in shelters is obvious: They can recycle a purebred, thereby doing the right thing *and* having the precise breed of their choice. There's an advantage for mutt lovers, too: Breed-specific rescue groups frequently have mixes available for adoption whose dominant component is that breed.

> An estimated 70,000 dogs and cats are born in the United States every day. In just six years, one intact female dog and her offspring can be the source of 67,000 puppies.

Mixed Breeds. The classic mutt, the mixed-breed dog is the one you most often see at your local shelter. Most mutts are accidents, and when accidents happen, people are caught unprepared. If you are faced with a litter of four or more dogs, what are you going to do? The right thing, if you can't take care of the mutts, is to find them good homes, or turn them

over to a shelter whose staff will try to do that for you.

Strays. Strays are homeless dogs, usually mixed breed. They may have had a loving family at one time and gotten lost. They may have been abandoned. They may have never had a family. Strays are usually captured by a caring person or dog warden and taken to a local shelter for care.

Abused Dogs. Pure or mixed, some dogs have the misfortune of falling into the wrong hands. Many abused dogs are rehabilitated. The worst cases are put down. The shelter will offer for adoption only dogs that can be rehabilitated or are already on their way to rehabilitation.

Handicapped Dogs. Dogs who are missing an eye or a limb or who have other physical flaws can be hard to place, so they often languish in shelters. Don't judge a dog by the leg count, though. These animals are some of the hardiest and most loving in the bunch.

LYNDA BARRY

THE MUTT CONUNDRUM

Dogs are not purists when it comes to romance; a purebred such as Lynda Barry's "Fred Milton, Beat Poodle" will often fall hard for a mutt (a good argument for spaying and neutering).

Mutts are born of parents who are intact (not spayed or neutered), yet mutt advocates endorse spaying and neutering. Mutts wouldn't exist if everyone spayed and neutered, so isn't it counterintuitive to recommend population control if you love mutts? Not at all. In addition to controlling the animal population, spaying and neutering is good for a dog's health. Spayed and neutered animals live longer, healthier lives. Neutered dogs have a decreased chance of developing prostate disease and are also less likely to stray from home. Spaying reduces the rate of breast cancer in female dogs. Spaying and neutering also help to eliminate many of the common behavioral problems that result in dogs being turned in to shelters, such as aggression or a tendency to wander and get lost. So if spaying and neutering is a must, why is it okay for people like the queen of England—who, in addition to breeding corgis, has bred dorgis (dachshunds and corgis)—to mate her dogs and not for me? Let's put it bluntly: Her Royal Highness is worth approximately $600 million, and she makes sure those pups are all well taken care of for the rest of their lives. Her dogs, pure or not, run no risk of falling into circumstances that could land them at an animal shelter (or refuge, as it's called in England). So unless you can absolutely guarantee the same lush life for every last one of your dog's litter, please spay and neuter.

Bittersweet Surrender

If something happens in your life and you absolutely cannot keep your mutt, you have three choices. You can find her a new home yourself; you can place her with a rescue organization; or you can surrender her to your local animal shelter.

If you opt for the first, try to place her with friends or someone whose references you've checked and double-checked. Do not place an advertisement in the local newspaper saying, "Free to good home." Very bad people keep their eyes peeled for such ads, posing as "good homes." They then turn around and sell the animal to a medical lab or other testing facility (these creeps are called Class C animal dealers). If you transfer ownership of your dog to a friend (or a reliable stranger), make sure you also handle the paperwork. The dog's microchip information, encoded on a computer chip that's injected under her skin (see page 46), should be updated (go to www.homeagainid.com or www.avidmicrochip.com for information). If you are not able to find a family yourself, a rescue organization is a good alter-native. If your budget allows, offer to make a donation to sponsor the dog's board while the rescue group works to find her a home. If neither of these options is available, the only right thing to do is to bring the dog to your local animal shelter, where the staff will be careful about checking potential adopters' backgrounds and references.

TOP 10 EXCUSES GIVEN FOR SURRENDERING A DOG TO A SHELTER

1. DIVORCE
2. FAMILY IS MOVING
3. DOG'S POOR BEHAVIOR/LACK OF TRAINING
4. LOSS OF INTEREST
5. LOSS OF JOB
6. DOG WRECKS FURNITURE
7. DOG DOESN'T MATCH NEW FURNITURE (!)
8. ALLERGIES
9. NEW BABY ON THE WAY
10. ELDERLY OWNER MOVES TO NURSING HOME

Helter Shelter

Animal shelters go by different names in different regions of the country. A shelter can be called Animal Control, the Humane Society, or SPCA (Society for the Prevention of Cruelty to Animals). Note that the ASPCA, for American Society for the Prevention of Cruelty to Animals, is different. It's a national humane organization based in New York City that was founded in 1866 and also operates a shelter. The charters of local SPCAs are similar to that of the ASPCA, and some regional SPCAs receive grant money from the "A," as insiders call it, but they are independent.

Some shelters receive government funding, so they are required to accept all animals brought to them. Obviously, that's a lot of dogs and cats. Space is limited, and there are always more dogs than there are people looking to adopt. The over-flow—usually those who have been in

residence the longest, or those deemed unadoptable—is euthanized, killed by a humane lethal injection of phenobarbital. Depending on the location and capacity of the kill shelter, a mutt's time can be as long as a month—or, in crowded urban shelters, as short as an hour.

Nongovernment-funded shelters operate on charitable donations; because they are not government subsidized, they can refuse to accept animals when they are at capacity, and sometimes they can afford not to kill animals. Some of these privately funded shelters have folksy names like Bide-A-Wee, which is Scots for "stay a while," and ARF (Animal Rescue Foundation).

Kill and no-kill shelters both are characterized by small numbers of overworked employees sometimes assisted by volunteers. Food and supplies are purchased from a shelter's small budget, and extras—including anything from towels to treats—are donated by local businesses and individuals. As many as eight million homeless dogs and cats are euthanized annually in this country's estimated six thousand animal shelters. The triage involved in deciding who is or isn't killed is not for the faint of heart; the job of shelter manager is one of the toughest imaginable.

> Obviously, the pressure is on at a kill shelter. We're talking *Schindler's List.*

Obviously, the pressure is on at a kill shelter. We're talking *Schindler's List.* If you hesitate, the dog you're attracted to today could be euthanized overnight (this happened to me once, and I confess I'm still not over it). If you feel a love connection with a dog, you'll have to take him or risk losing him forever. Mutts adopted from kill shelters, I've found, really know what you've done for them. They have profound soul; they are grateful. No dog who hasn't spent time in a shelter will ever have that dimension to her personality. The silver lining of kill shelters is that dogs haven't been in residence very long, so they haven't had a chance to become dejected. They're still upbeat and hopeful of getting sprung, so once you've brought them home, you won't have to wait for layers of worry to melt away.

At no-kill shelters, there's no pressure that a dog will lose her life imminently if you don't adopt her and take her home that day. So if you're the type who needs to deliberate when it comes to making any decision, you can go back and visit several times and really think about which dog to take (the only "risk" being

Hearts of stone could melt upon entering a shelter and hearing the din of barking, leaping, frantic mutts all trying to get your attention. If you're like me, you will want to cry. Please resist. Recalling her trips abroad with the late Bob Hope to spread cheer to American troops stationed overseas, comedienne Phyllis Diller described the time she saw a hospitalized young soldier in very bad shape. Without thinking, she burst into tears, whereupon Hope took her aside and gave her a stern talking-to about keeping things light. The same goes for shelters. Being caged is upsetting enough for the dogs, so accentuate the positive. Coo gently at them, and stay upbeat. Even if you can't take all the mutts home with you that day, you can look at them kindly and smile.

Copious quantities of unconditional love are on offer at your local animal shelter.

Cared for by a revolving cast of staffers, volunteers, and foster caregivers, dogs can develop an understandable reluctance to become deeply attached to any one human. When this happens, a dog may come to regard anyone who shows up to take her out as just another person on duty. Even after you bring a shelter veteran home, you may have to wait patiently for a couple of weeks for the bonding process to start.

In addition to shelters, good mutt matches can be made through a couple of other tried-and-true means:

Petfinder.com. Since its 1995 launch, www.petfinder.com has revolutionized pet adoption, making it easy and efficient. It's not a shelter; it's a nationwide

that a more fast-acting person might adopt the dog you were interested in). There is one caveat, however: If a dog has been languishing unadopted at a no-kill shelter for a year or more (not unheard of), she could become shelter-shocked.

listing of animals available for adoption at shelters across the country, with vital stats on each dog and often a photo—even such valuable information as whether the dog is good with other pets or children—all details that help enormously in narrowing down your choice. It's absolutely painless to use; in fact, many mutt lovers have been known to while away recreational hours just looking at the adorable dogs featured on the site. You can search by zip code, by type of animal, or, in the case of dogs, by breed. Petfinder has been instrumental in enabling mutt people to connect with the precise type of mixed breed they are looking for, making the hunt for the ideal mutt as exact a science as possible. Some people won't hesitate to travel hundreds of miles, passing numerous animal shelters along the way, to get to a mutt they're smitten with. Rescued purebreds are underdogs as much as mutts, and

Petfinder is also an excellent resource for connecting with them. If there's a particular breed you fancy, type that breed into Petfinder's search field, and you'll see the available mixes whose dominant component is that breed.

Breed Rescue Groups. There is a breed rescue group for almost every breed of dog. These are tight-knit, loyal networks of people who take care of their own. Dogs are fostered by volunteer families until homes can be found. Just type the breed of your choice plus the word "rescue" into any Web search engine (like "dalmatian rescue"), and you'll pull up all the information you need. (My favorite search engine is www.dogpile.com, for obvious reasons.)

Not Growling, Smiling

Many caged mutts will smile at you, so excited are they to greet visitors. Those smiles are called "submissive grins" but sometimes they—and the sneezes and snorts that may accompany them—are misunderstood as menacing teeth-baring, especially in shepherd or pit mixes. Recognize bared teeth in this context as a happy overture, and give a smiling mutt a chance.

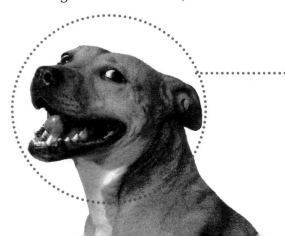

CRYING WOLF

There is a growing market for wolf "hybrids," animals that are part dog and part wolf. These animals are not mutts; they are the products of unscrupulous breeding. Some people buy them in order to project a macho image but soon become overwhelmed by the care the animals require. "Wolf dogs consume one hundred percent of your time," explains Art Bellis of Wolfsong Ranch Foundation in New Mexico, a haven for wolf dogs whose people gave up on them. "You can't leave them in the house; you need a big, fenced-in compound. They're not like children, where you can get someone else to baby-sit. These are pack animals, so if you leave them alone, they become neurotic. They really suffer. And they're not like ordinary dogs: Small animals, including cats, and anything that looks like a rabbit, are on their menu." The majority of wolf dogs don't live past eighteen months old: They are shot by frustrated owners, or turned loose, only to be killed by hunters or picked up and euthanized by animal control (it's illegal for shelters to adopt out wolf dogs). For those who still want to have a wolf dog in their lives, Wolfsong offers this humane compromise: For a $250 tax-deductible donation, which goes toward the care and feeding of rescued wolf dogs, you can "adopt" one of the sanctuary's 187 residents—but that animal never leaves the sanctuary. It's just like adopting a highway, only fiercer and fuzzier.

For several years, social-awareness stamps issued by the United States Postal Service have been successful in getting the public talking about important issues such as breast cancer and organ donation. Animal lovers across the country spent five years diligently petitioning the Citizens Stamp Advisory Committee (a group of independent citizens appointed by the Postmaster General to review the more than forty thousand suggestions for stamp subjects the Postal Service receives each year), requesting a stamp design that would draw attention to the serious problem of pet overpopulation. The letter-writing campaign drew the participation of major animal-welfare groups such as the Humane Society of the United States, the ASPCA, and the Doris Day Animal League. Something about the persistence of mutt advocates (shelter cats are mutts, too) struck a chord with the CSAC in 2001, because in October of that year it was announced that not one, but two "spay/neuter" first-class commemorative stamps would finally be issued. One featured a spayed kitten named Samantha, and the other, a neutered collie-shepherd mix named Kirby.

RECEIPT

No. 590902

DATE 05/24/05 $250.00

RECEIVED FROM KRISTY SUMMERS

TWO HUNDRED FIFTY ———————— DOLLARS

FOR RENT / FOR TAX-DEDUCTIBLE DONATION TO WOLFSONG

FROM KRISTY SUMMERS TO WOLFSONG

ACCOUNT   ☐ CASH
PAYMENT   ☑ CHECK
BAL. DUE   ☐ MONEY ORDER   BY

FIRST CLASS

Shelter Outreach

To encourage adoptions, more and more shelters across the country are getting creative, reaching out with fun-filled events to match people with homeless pets. It's all about creative marketing. Making pet adoption as easy as a recreational

The Mighty Mutts table at the Mayor's Alliance for NYC's Animals summer adopt-a-thon in Manhattan's Central Park.

shopping spree, PETsMART has facilitated the placement of more than 1.5 million homeless pets, dedicating space in every store to some 2,400 animal welfare organizations. Smaller pet supply boutiques and doggie day care facilities also frequently yield space to local shelters and animal rescue groups to call attention to mutts needing homes. On the theory that women tend to gravitate to fashion and men to athletics, that singles are looking to meet a mate, and that everyone loves to eat, shelter-outreach events combine these draws with mutt adoption to cover

all bases, staging mutt runway shows, walk-a-thons or other outdoorsy events (Utah's annual Strut Your Mutt; the Nob Hill Pooch Parade in Albuquerque, New Mexico; or Portland, Oregon's annual Doggie Dash), Valentine's Day mixers, and picnics. Other shelters organize radio adopt-a-thons and TV "adoptelethons," "Santa Paws" photo opportunities at holiday time, or pet photo contests, where people pay a $1 donation to vote. In New York City, the Brooklyn Animal Resource Coalition (BARC) sponsors an annual Halloween parade showcasing eligible adoptables and offering prizes for the most imaginative canine costumes. Blue Dog Rescue of Austin, Texas, has two benefits every year: a Perros de Mayo festival (Spanish for Dogs of May, a reference to the Mexican holiday Cinco de Mayo) and "Dogtoberfest," complete with beer and refreshments reminiscent of Bavaria's autumnal Oktoberfest. For film buffs, there's DogFest, the annual all-canine underground short film festival. Entries, no longer than five minutes, must be about a dog or have canines as central characters. Events like these become highly anticipated traditions in their respective communities.

Some adoption events are quite posh affairs involving fancy invitations, high admission prices, cocktails, catered food, auctions, raffles, and usually a catchy name, like the annual Lint Roller Party and Save a Stray Soiree, sponsored by No More Homeless Pets in Utah. North Carolina's Wake County SPCA and the San Diego, California, Humane Society both host an event called the Fur Ball. In Philadelphia, the Pennsylvania SPCA benefits from DogHaus, the first-ever decorator showhouse to benefit shelter animals. It proves that a house isn't a home until a mutt lives there.

Creative ways to volunteer

At a New York-based animal volunteer group, Critter Knitters Coalition, crafty folks with varying degrees of skill in knitting, crocheting, and sewing create blankets for shelter pets to help cozy up their cages while they await adoption. As it happens, an animal is more likely to be adopted if she has a blanket in her cage, a phenomenon that struck the mother of all "critter knitters," Rae French of Hugs for Homeless Animals, who founded The Snuggles Project in 1996. Meanwhile, Los Angeles schoolteacher Robin Roth, an editor of the Web site www.arkonline.com, educates her students at Palos Verdes Peninsula High about animal welfare, frequently pointing to the teacher's pet: her mutt, Bingo. Duly inspired, Roth's students organized a holiday drive on behalf of homeless animals, bringing donated pet food, dog toys, and blankets to a group called SPARE (Save Pound Animals through Rescue and Education) for distribution at local animal shelters.

(((Shelter-Shocked)))

In 1994 I met **Daisy,** a pit bull–dalmatian cross, at New York City's ASPCA (a no-kill shelter). When I first saw her, she'd been living in a cage for several months. When I finally made the decision to adopt her and bring her home—the first dog I'd had since my childhood—I was ecstatic.

Daisy, less so. She walked out with one of the handlers and yawned in my face. Evidently, for her this did not have the makings of a momentous event. She thought we were just going out for a little walk. After I helped her into a taxicab for the ride home, she focused her gaze on the window, showing me her back for the entire ride. I'll never forget how underwhelmed she was to be going home. After about a month, however, I'm pleased to report that Daisy's nonchalant mask fell, and her uncontrollable smiling and sneezing when I came home let me know that she was, in fact, happy to be mine (smiling with joy often causes dogs to sneeze). If I hadn't been patient, I might have returned Daisy to the shelter for being less affectionate than I'd hoped she would be. The moral: Give mutts

The late, great Daisy in full-throttle Santa Paws mode.

time. They will rise to the occasion and reward you for your patience, sooner or later. Daisy rewarded me with every young writer's dream: an appearance in *The New Yorker*. Like so many stories I was to write later, it was all about Daisy (to read it, just turn the page).

The story of a shopping hound

On a long Saturday night at the Animal Medical Center, on East 62nd Street, there was nothing to do but worry, wait, and read an underrated magazine called *Pethouse*. In it was an article entitled "Shopping with Your Dog," which listed the various Upper East Side stores that welcome customers *mit Hund*. This is all well and good for pugs such as Eloise's Weenie and other lap breeds indigenous to Fifth and Park Avenues— Yorkie, Jack Russell, papillon—but what about a pit bull–dalmatian named Daisy?

Alfred Dunhill

When Daisy goes for a walk, she induces the usual reactions occasioned by the passing of a gorgeous female: Boys gawk, men do double takes, women of all ages tend to look the other way. Daisy is famous in her Murray Hill neighborhood for her white coat, kohl-rimmed brown eyes, snowy lashes, husky frame, and gentle disposition—the sum of these parts suggesting a polar bear crossed with a cow.

Louis Vuitton

At Bergdorf's, Daisy received precisely the unconditional welcome that *Pethouse* had guaranteed, submitting patiently as she was fitted with a brown pincord coat by George, the San Francisco–based pet outfitters, and gazing with admirably restrained lust upon a display bed dressed in Pratesi linens. But, being a dog who enjoys playfully half-nelsoning males twice her

F.A.O. Schwarz

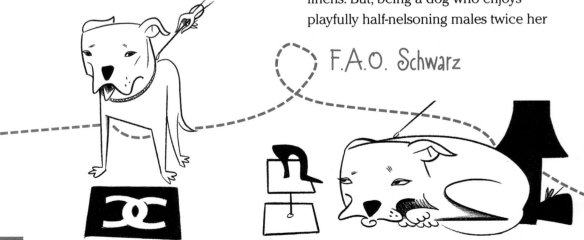

size, Daisy was up for the challenge of gaining access to a few stores not on the *Pethouse* list: Alfred Dunhill, Buccellati, Louis Vuitton (no problem), Prada (where she resisted any residual urge to chew shoes), Hermès (where no fewer than four silk-scarved vendeuses fawned over her), Chanel (the doorman didn't blink), and Tiffany (where a security guard was overheard registering "woman with large dog" on his walkie-talkie). At the uptown branch of Barneys, store policy dictates that all dogs be carried, and Daisy's fifty-four pounds made this a daunting proposition for her hundred-and-seven-pound handler. The same scenario greeted Daisy at F.A.O. Schwarz and Henri Bendel. This last stop was especially sobering because Henri Bendel the younger—the nephew of the original, who is now captain of the Belgian Shoes

Hermès

Tiffany

Prada

Henri Bendel

shop—remembers a time when certain Fifth Avenue stores provided drinking fountains for canine visitors.

Finally, it was time to head downtown and on to ABC Carpet & Home for a long overdue survey of the Herman Miller for the Home collection. Just shy of the ABC threshold, Daisy put on a look of horrified alarm and began to take two steps backward for every one forward. The cause of her never-before-witnessed behavior turned out to be two stone lions guarding the entrance; while not exactly Patience and Fortitude, they were evidently efficient in the dispatch of their duty. Once inside, Daisy met with no requests to leave, so she sniffed around in the lighting department, where she was promptly ambushed by a snarling dachshund belonging to a sales associate.

The End

R i s k o

The Adoption Process

No need to stand on ceremony or make an appointment when you set out to adopt your mutt. Just find out the hours of your local animal shelter—most are open seven days a week—and show up. If you have children, bring them along. When you arrive, tell the person at reception you are interested in adopting.

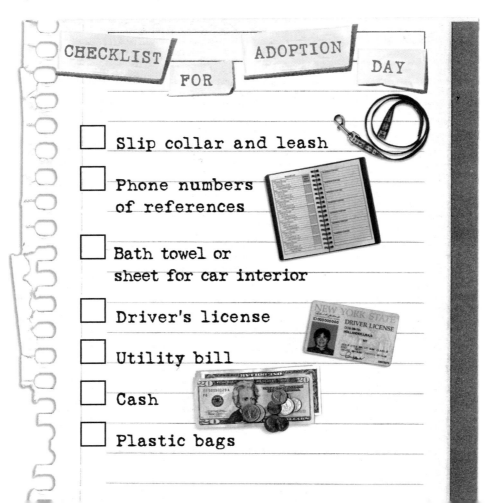

CHECKLIST FOR ADOPTION DAY

- ☐ Slip collar and leash
- ☐ Phone numbers of references
- ☐ Bath towel or sheet for car interior
- ☐ Driver's license
- ☐ Utility bill
- ☐ Cash
- ☐ Plastic bags

Some shelters require you to fill out paperwork before you even meet the dogs. The application process involves an interview and checking of references, which might include friends and a veterinarian (if you already have a pet). If you rent your home, bring a copy of your lease proving that dogs are allowed in the apartment. Bring photo ID and proof of address, like a utility bill. You will be asked to sign an adoption agreement, a contract that holds you to the promise that, among other things, you will provide food, water, exercise, shelter, and medical care for the animal, and that you will never turn around and sell your mutt to a research facility for animal testing. Some shelters may require a home check also. Do not feel offended by what may seem like shelter staffers giving you the third degree or micromanaging you; it's not personal. It's just that they've seen a lot of mistreated mutts in very bad situations, so they naturally want to be sure that nothing bad ever happens to the mutts now in their care. Checking references and being careful is good for all mutts, so be patient.

When you're cleared to adopt, be prepared with money for the adoption fee, which goes toward the shelter's expenses

THE MUTT COST OF LIVING

Adopting a dog is not just an emotional commitment; it's a financial commitment. In its annual "Cost of a Dog" report, the British insurer Churchill calculated that dog-care costs for the average dog total 20,000 pounds over the course of the animal's lifetime (almost $38,000). This was based on the three basics of dog care: food, veterinary care, and grooming. Of course, the incidentals will also add up: day care, boarding while you travel, and supplies, including chew toys and other playthings, training crates, and so forth. Also, keep in mind that large dogs cost more than small ones. Churchill calculated that the lifetime cost of a Great Dane (a giant breed that can reach 150 to 200 pounds) is 31,840 pounds ($60,000).

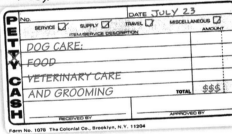

of maintaining all the dogs in its care. Remember that the shelter has put a great deal of effort and money into deworming, vaccinating, neutering, in many instances microchipping, and generally caring for the mutt you're about to take home. Adoption fees vary, so call ahead or come prepared with $100 to $200. You might also consider bringing extra money to make a tax-deductible donation to help the shelter keep up the good work. If you grumble about the adoption fee, then you're in no financial position to care for a mutt. Mutt care costs money over the long haul. If you haven't already, you should budget for basic expenses such as food, then set aside a reserve fund of at least $1,000 for emergency veterinary care.

You'll be shown into the area where the cages are. Always visit with the mutts you're considering outside of their cages. Most shelters have small dog runs or get-acquainted rooms for this purpose, because as soon as they're outside of their cages, dogs reveal their true personalities. Think about it: How would you feel if you were cooped up in a cage at a dark, noisy animal shelter, with your fellow inmates barking and howling nonstop? Probably more than a little depressed, anxious, or outright terrified. If you've been in residence there a long time, passed over by dozens of people, you've come to feel thoroughly demoralized. How a dog behaves in his cage is not an accurate barometer of his character; some dogs appear shy but emerge from their shells outside, while others are ultra-vocal when caged but much quieter uncaged.

Foster Mutt

If you can't have a dog right now, consider becoming a foster parent. If your schedule and living arrangement permit you to take care of a dog for the short term—say, a month or two—you can foster a mutt in your home. Here's how it works: You act as that mutt's temporary guardian; he lives with you while you help the shelter arrange to introduce him to potential adopters until he gets a permanent home. Fostering helps open up cage space at the shelter for more dogs and allows the mutt being fostered to feel more relaxed, free of the stress of the shelter environment. It's also a great way for anyone who's never had a dog before to test the waters and see if adoption is right for her. If you cannot foster a dog, you can still volunteer in other ways, like photographing shelter dogs with your digital camera and writing captivating adoption notices, walking shelter dogs, and helping the local shelter with its Web site.

NAME THAT MUTT

Ellen DeGeneres hosts a popular daytime talk show with millions of viewers, so back in September 2003, when she was naming her adorable mutt puppy, she enlisted their help in voting on the pup's name, which ended up being Lucy.

Umlaut the batard was collectively named by the readers of the Internet poetry gazette EVerseRadio.

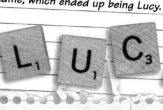

MUTT'S IN A NAME?

Often, mutts come prenamed; like the colorful bandannas you sometimes see on shelter dogs, a memorable moniker is the animal shelter's way of highlighting a mutt's irresistible uniqueness. But let's say you can't stand the name a mutt comes with. Naturally, you can always change it—remember, adaptability (not to mention adoptability) is a mixed-breed forte. My own mutts all have at least three or four different nicknames, and they're not alone. Remember Hank Azaria's character, Nat, on the late, great sitcom Mad About You, who was always coming up with witty alternative handles for Murray the mutt? The list was long, and the names were frequently improvised by the actor: Furry Murray, Murray Tyler Moore, Murray Slaughter, Virgin Murray, Murray Magdalene, Murray Antoinette, Murray Osmond, Murray-Lu Henner, F. Murray Abraham, Bill Murray, Fred MacMurray, Murray Queen of Scots, RoseMurray's Baby, Murray Murray Quite Contrary . . . So go ahead and rename that mutt. Your one-of-a-kind dog deserves an equally unique handle.

I LOVE U

Marcelle Furrow-Kiebler, a teacher, moved with her husband from California to Provence, where she learned of the French regulation requiring that animals be named alphabetically by year (1983 was the letter A, 1984 was B, and so on; the next cycle begins in 2008, when it's back to A). "The idea is that you know the age of an animal if you know his name," she explains. "This is more important to breeders and farmers than to your average person, but the regulation applies to everyone." When the couple adopted a female batard, a Brittany spaniel–griffon mix, at a foire aux chiens (dog fair) in Provence in 2003, the year of the U, they were stumped for a creative U name. So they put the word out on EVerseRadio, an Internet poetry gazette. Being a witty, literate bunch, the EVersers came up with . . . Umlaut.

I've Got You Under My Skin

Collars and tags can fall off, so dogs require some form of permanent identification. The low-tech form of permanent ID is a tattoo; the high-tech version is a microchip. A dog who's been microchipped has been pricked by a needle, except instead of an inoculation or a medication, what's inserted under the skin is a computer chip the size of a rice grain containing vital information: the pet's home address and telephone number, or the address and number of the shelter she was adopted from, plus alternate contacts. This way, if the animal becomes lost, she can be scanned with an electronic scanning device to reveal vital information that could help her find her way home.

If the dog later changes hands, it is up to the person relinquishing the dog to a new guardian to have the microchip data updated. One microchip is called, appropriately, Home Again, and the database that houses the information on the microchip is run by the AKC. Yes, the organization dedicated to purebred dogs deserves praise for recognizing that all animals are created equal when it comes to keeping pets safe and reuniting them with their people if they become lost. AKC Companion Animal Recovery is a wonderfully inclusive nonprofit 501(c)(3) organization dedicated to providing lifetime recovery services for all microchipped animals, serving as a central registry where a pet's microchip ID number is safely stored and used to contact the owner when the pet is reported found. The fee of just $12.50 per pet

> The low-tech form of permanent ID is a tattoo; the high-tech version is a microchip.

includes lifetime recovery services, and for your peace of mind, the toll-free hotline, 800-252-7894, is manned around the clock: 24 hours a day, 7 days a week, 365 days a year. AKC/CAR does a recovery every eight minutes.

At press time, more than 2.7 million pets were enrolled and more than 258,000 had been returned home. If you come across a stray that you might want to adopt, the first thing you should do (after having her checked by a vet) is have her scanned for a microchip at the animal shelter nearest you; animal shelters can contact Home Again and request to receive a free scanner for this purpose. Someone might be out there at wits' end, frantically searching for this dog. The microchip will enable you to orchestrate a happy reunion.

Where am I?
Who are you?

Please bring me to my friends!

The Way to Save a Stray

Not everyone finds an underdog. Sometimes, the dog finds them. A mutt may adopt you if he crosses your path as a stray, if he's tied to a fence in the middle of nowhere or standing alone in the dog run waiting for a person who isn't coming back; he could be wandering by the side of a deserted country road; he could be dodging traffic in the middle of a busy urban intersection. He might be calm and come right to you wagging his tail, or he might elude capture by running away. Taking animal rescue into your own hands is a difficult, frustrating, and sometimes dangerous undertaking. Here's how to do it safely.

Call for help. If the situation is simply too dangerous for you to get involved directly, call directory assistance and ask to be connected to animal control or the local police precinct. Remain at the scene so you can direct the officers to the animal. It's especially important to get help if a dog is injured.

Assume a nonthreatening position. If you decide to try to capture the dog yourself, remember that most strays are frightened. Your body language and tone of voice are critical. Crouch down as low as possible and try not to move or make eye contact. Keep your palms upturned and your voice reassuring.

Call to the dog. Talk slowly and softly in a soothing, beckoning voice—"Here, puppy!"—and use your upper vocal register to avoid using low tones that might sound like a growl.

Offer food. If you happen to have food on you, do offer it. Hunger may enable a dog to overcome his fear.

Don't chase the dog. He could end up in traffic or run away.

Make a slip lead. Use whatever you've got handy—a belt, piece of twine, or extension cord (don't use a bungee cord, as it can snap with great force, causing serious injury to the dog and you). If the dog growls, tucks his tail under his legs, or puts his ears all the way back, stay away, as he may bite.

Lift her into your car. If the dog is hurt, drive to animal control, an animal emergency hospital, or a police station. If she looks healthy, you can take her home with you until you can get her looked at by a vet.

Keep him separated. If you already have pets at home, keep them away from the stray until you know the dog's health status (he could be worm or flea infested).

The stray might also be aggressive toward other animals even if he's good with people.

SPOT
212 555 3311

Search for ID. Take the dog to the vet and search for a tattoo or microchip. If you'd like to keep the dog, do your due diligence in putting up "found dog" signs with your phone number. Someone out there might be desperately looking for this dog. If, despite all that, the dog turns out to be homeless and if no one comes forward to claim him, you can keep him or surrender him to your local animal shelter.

HERE DOGGIE, DOGGIE

Animal experts agree that small cans of cat food work wonders when coaxing stray dogs to safety; the pungent aroma is a big draw. "I always carry cat food," says Ingrid Newkirk, president of People for the Ethical Treatment of Animals (PETA). "If you carry just one small can, it will fit into the tiniest purse or the glove compartment of your car or your bicycle bag."

DOG TIMES

CELEB SAVES STRAY

One night in November 2003, actor Eric Stoltz noticed a stray dog running onto the off-ramp of a busy highway. He pulled over to help. He tried luring the dog to safety with a Luna bar, which did not inspire the animal. Luckily, another motorist stopped to offer the dog a can of cat food, "which he went ape for," Stoltz says. It was 11:20 at night, cars were honking, and the dog was frantic, but finally the adorable shepherd-rottweiler-pit bull-Lab landed safely in Stoltz's station wagon. "It took about forty-five minutes to lure him to the car," the actor says. "Then he calmed down."

The stray had a collar, but no tags. What if he hadn't been abandoned, but had accidentally become separated from his people, who might be frantically searching for him? To be sure, Stoltz took the dog to a vet to have him scanned for a microchip, but the scan revealed no ID. Happily, the vet's exam showed there was nothing wrong with the dog other than dehydration. The lucky mutt earned himself the name Chancer—an Irish term for "someone who takes great risks, pushes his luck, and survives," Stoltz explains. The name fit. After inquiring at area shelters and finding that all have kill policies due to lack of space, Stoltz decided to manage Chancer's adoption himself. He had the dog neutered and vaccinated, and began training Chancer in the basics. "He was so eager to please, he learned to sit in a day," he says. A couple of months later, Chancer found a home.

Actor-director-producer Eric Stoltz with Chancer, the mutt he rescued from a Los Angeles freeway.

Black Is Beautiful

Strangely, even in New York and other cities where black is *the* fashion color, people who wear head-to-toe black tend to gravitate toward mutts with pale coats (which is ridiculously impractical given the shedding issue; at least black hairs are less obvious on black clothing).

Joking aside, it's a matter of discrimination. Black mutts really do experience prejudice. Some Mutt Mavens, like Kimora Lee Simmons, adopt only black animals, yet all-black or predominantly black animals are routinely passed over at animal shelters across the country in favor of dogs that have lighter coats. Some rescue groups will not accept black dogs into their adoption programs because it is so difficult to find them a home, especially the black males (they are somehow viewed as more menacing than females). As a result, the majority of black mutts in this country wind up euthanized. To help even out the odds, www.petfinder.com runs a banner that reads, "Did you know . . . that large, black dogs are often the last to be adopted? Think big, adopt big." Shelters across the country experience the same phenomenon. "At least 80 percent of our dog kennel is black 98 percent of the time," says Katherine Christenson of Georgia's Atlanta Humane Society. "People always take the blond dogs first;

Beautiful Jackie stayed at the Humane Society of New York for more than a year—until designer Todd Oldham took this portrait. Shortly after, she found a home.

it's horrible." Compounding the problem, shelters tend to be dark and poorly lit, so black animals are difficult to see. And black dogs can be very tricky to photograph clearly, so at shelters that operate Web sites, often all you can see in photos of black dogs are their eyes. Things get worse in October: The ancient superstition that black animals bring bad luck lingers, especially in the days leading up to Halloween. But October also happens to be Adopt-a-Shelter-Dog Month, and staffers at animal shelters around the country keep hoping that potential adopters can over-come lingering, irrational fears and let a beautiful black dog steal their heart. "Not being able to look past the color of an animal's coat is like not being able to look past the color of a per-son's skin," says William Berloni of the Humane Society of New York. And mutt lovers are better than that, aren't we?

READY FOR HER CLOSE-UP

Jackie, a black shepherd mix, waited patiently at the Humane Society of New York for more than a year before going home; according to the shelter, that's twice as long as the average stay for a dog who isn't black. To draw attention to the plight of black dogs in general, and Jackie in particular, the designer-photographer-filmmaker Todd Oldham shot Jackie's portrait in a glamorous style reminiscent of George Hurrell, famed for his photographs of 1930s Hollywood stars. Jackie was adopted not long after that—after all, she'd become a fashion model!

Regional tribes

Although mutts of all descriptions turn up everywhere, certain types of mutts tend to predominate in certain areas of the country.

NORTH

Mixes of retriever, shepherd, Malamute, and husky

WEST

Cattle dog, border collie, Australian shepherd, and rottweiler mixes

EAST

Pit bull, rottweiler, retriever, beagle, and dalmatian mixes

URBAN AREAS

German shepherd, pit bull, chow, Chihuahua, and rottweiler mixes

SOUTH

Hound, pit bull, border collie, pointer, and spaniel mixes

MIDWEST

Mixes whose dominant ingredient is a pet shop purebred, due to the proliferation of puppy mills in this region

Designer Mutts

ne of the many things that makes mutts mutts is that they are not available at pet stores; you have to find them as strays on the street or adopt them from an animal shelter. Now, believe it or not, greedy breeders have begun trying to cash in on mixed-breed chic. Of late, pet shops have been touting designer hybrids, including the cockapoo (a cocker spaniel–poodle cross), the schnoodle (a schnauzer-poodle); the Pekapoo (a Pekingese-poodle), the Pekapom (a Pekingese-Pomeranian), and the Pomalier (a Pomeranian–Cavalier King Charles spaniel).

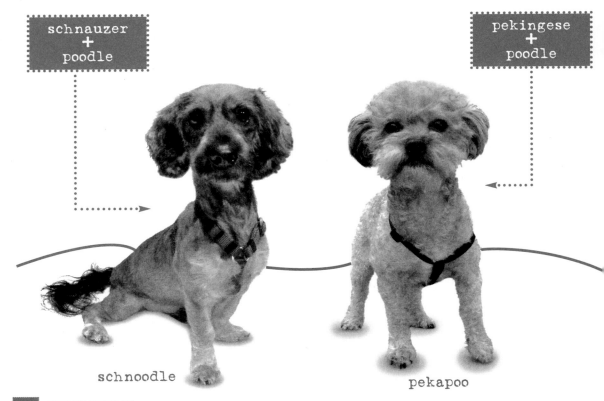

schnauzer
+
poodle

pekingese
+
poodle

schnoodle

pekapoo

These are not AKC-recognized breeds, yet pet stores charge as much as $1,500 for these pups. Ethicists and mutt lovers agree it's preferable to go to a shelter and adopt a homeless mixed breed rather than support a business that creates new mixed-breed dogs for sale.

On doodles

The beauty of mutts is that they happen unscientifically. But there is one dog not recognized by the AKC that's the result of more than thirty years of careful research and development. Somewhere in dog limbo, the Labradoodle is neither mutt nor AKC-recognized purebred. In 1970, Australian Wally Cochran created the Labradoodle, doodle for short, by crossing a Labrador retriever and a standard poodle; his goal was to enable blind people who were allergic to dogs to have guide dogs that wouldn't cause them physical discomfort (poodle fur is more easily tolerated by people who are allergic to dog dander). Combining the Lab's trainability and willingness to please with the poodle's high intelligence and non-shedding coat, the doodle has become

Life magazine launched a run on doodles in 2004.

quite popular as a family pet down under and here in the United States, as the numerous Americans waiting expectantly for Tegan Park and Rutland Manor (two Aussie breeders) doodle pups at Los Angeles Airport's Qantas terminal can attest. And since the Labradoodle is not recognized by the AKC, it wouldn't be a stretch to call him an honorary mutt. But really, why go to all that trouble and expense when there are so many Lab and poodle mixes right on these shores, at a shelter near you? No dog is truly hypoallergenic—they all have dander, whether purebred or mixed—and as we'll see later, there are ways even for allergy sufferers to live with a beloved mutt.

Mixology:

The Mutt Family Tree

cyn•ol•o•gy /sin-ol-o-je/ n. the study of purebred dogs.

mix•ol•o•gy /mik-sol-o-je/ n. the study of mutts.

The study of purebred dogs is called cynology, so it seems only fitting to invent a study of mutts and call it mixology. The potential combinations that can result when two dogs of different breeds mate are astonishingly various; mutts are more than the sums of their parts. Sometimes, a mutt looks a great deal like one of the breeds that contributed to his makeup. Other times, there's no accounting for his appearance. Trying to identify a mutt's main ingredients is no small part of the fun of having one or admiring one from afar. Does she have the wiry coat and beard of a terrier on the big body of a Lab? The blue tongue of a chow chow? "Furnishings," or long hair on the extremities, like a border collie? A double-curled tail like an Akita or a Norwegian elkhound? The spotted, or "ticked," coat of a spaniel or pointer on the slender torso of a greyhound? The unmistakable, gravity-defying ears of a briard? Or the feathery drop ears and hairy paws of a spaniel?

Certain breeds have distinguishing physical characteristics that I like to call "bred giveaways." For instance, you can tell there's basset hound in a mutt if the dog is low to the ground and stands on dwarfy, wrinkly, turned-out legs. When one breed obviously predominates, the dog is referred to as a mix of that breed, like a German shepherd mix.

Chow mixes retain the regal, powerful appearance of their purebred cousins, yet all the ones I've met also have sweet, outgoing natures once you get to know them.

Playing the breed-identification game is much more than an elitist exercise in finding evidence of princely purebred roots in canine paupers. It's a valuable tool to understanding any mutt and the behaviors he's likely to demonstrate during your life together. The more you can decode about a mystery dog's origins from the way he looks, the more likely you'll be able to make a match with the ideal dog for your lifestyle, to give him the lifestyle he instinctively needs, and to

head off behavioral or health issues before they become problematic.

Often, a mix will look like one of the breeds that contributed to her makeup, but behave significantly differently. Purebreds were developed to display very intense behaviors, whether for hunting, guarding, or herding. In most cases, breeds with such intense traits are significantly mellowed by being mixed with one or more other breeds.

Purebred chow chows, for instance, tend to be reserved with strangers, in keeping with the purpose for which they were bred: guard duty. Many people are afraid of chow chows because of that aloofness combined with their appearance (large head, powerful jaw). The chow chow was developed in ancient China as a guard dog, and that guarding instinct remains in the dog to this day, so they are naturally protective of their owners, revealing their devotion to their family by being wary of strangers. However, when a chow chow is combined with another breed of dog, that defensive attitude is softened considerably—and frequently eradicated altogether—until the dog is an outgoing, cuddly bundle of fluff. Chow mixes retain the regal, powerful appearance of their purebred cousins, yet all the ones I've met also have sweet, outgoing natures once you get to know them.

If a mutt has drop ears like a beagle or other hunt-

Many mutts are so mellow that they cohabitate peaceably with cats, as Poko demonstrates with "her" pet kitten, Batmanuel.

ing hound, chances are he'll have a powerful hunting instinct in his mongrel makeup, so you'll want to be sure to use a leash at all times and work with him diligently on commands like "stay" and "come" so you have a shot at recovering him should he spontaneously race off in search of a squirrel.

If your mutt has the wiry coat or beard of a terrier, chances are she also possesses a good deal of the typical terrier's tenacity, intelligence, and love of rats and digging. Any mutt that looks like a dalmatian, with black spots on a white coat and on the fair skin beneath, will, like a purebred dalmatian, require

plenty of exercise. These spotted dogs were bred to run alongside coaches. When mixed with another type of dog, that born-to-run spirit will be somewhat subdued, but the spotted mutt will still have a need to stretch her legs, maybe vigorously so. If you're a jogger, even an occasional one, a dalmatian hybrid could be the perfect mutt for you. Even if you're not a runner but have the energy and dedication to take the mutt to a dog run every single day, where she can safely enjoy off-leash exercise, the match is still a great one. But if you're

If your mutt has the wiry coat or beard of a terrier, chances are she also possesses a good deal of the typical terrier's tenacity, intelligence, and love of rats and digging.

a dedicated couch potato, neither of you will find fulfillment.

Herding dogs were bred to help farmers and shepherds by rounding up livestock; they combine intelligence and agility as no other dog breeds do. Without livestock to herd, they will find other outlets for that instinct. In the absence of a job to do, mixes containing herding-dog genes—border collie mixes or corgi mixes, for instance—will gather up sofa cushions and shoes, and may even round up the kids, too, in an effort to keep everyone and everything safely in one place. Border collie mixes especially need lots of interaction to keep their intelligent minds and athletic bodies occupied. Frequent games of Frisbee and lots of kids to play with will go a long way to keeping your border collie mix happy.

Some mutts are so generous with kisses, hugs, and lap dances that to call them friendly would be an understatement. These are the serious affection hounds, and they need to have their love requited vigorously and often. Contrary to what you may have read or seen in sensationalist news stories, pit bulls are extremely affectionate creatures, and so are pit bull mixes. So if you'd rather not be smothered with kisses and licks, or if you just prefer a more reserved, aloof canine companion, this type of mutt won't be right for you.

Two of the most ubiquitous types of mix appearing in animal shelters are shepherd and Labrador mixes. Certain characteristics distinguish the shepherd and make him recognizable even to those who don't know very much about dogs. Shepherds have a long, dark snout, erect ears, a black-and-tan coat, and a long, large, athletic body. A shepherd mix, on the other hand, can be smaller than a purebred shepherd or, if mixed with an even larger breed, much bigger. You can expect a shepherd mix to be hardworking, intelligent, and very trainable.

Contrary to what you may have read or seen, pit bulls are extremely affectionate creatures, and so are pit bull mixes.

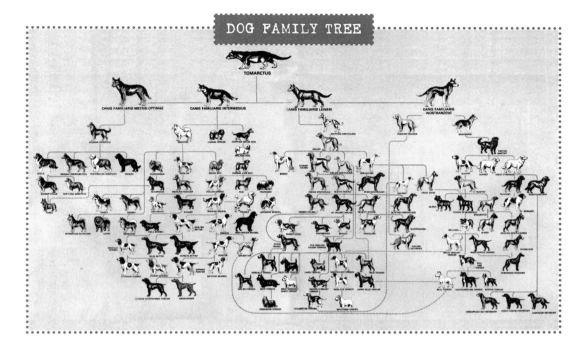

The Labrador retriever is as athletic as the shepherd, but she has drop ears and her head and snout are wide. A Lab mix's head, however, will often be narrower and her snout longer—unless she is mixed with, say, a pit bull, another breed distinguished by a broad head and wide snout. Instead of drop ears, she may have erect or semiprick ones. If a wire-haired terrier enters the mix, the Lab's glossy coat will take on a wiry consistency, and she will sport whiskers— if not a full beard. Give a Lab mix a regular outlet for exercise, or she is likely to grow bored. Labs are also natural-born swimmers, as are Lab mixes. Since water is their element, if you're lucky enough to have a pond or lake near you, your dog's fun and fitness are guaranteed if you take her for regular swims. Don't forget to bring along a toy that floats for your Lab mix to fetch—that retrieving instinct may still be there!

After several mixed breeds have mated over a period of time, the cross-pollinated traits of many different breeds start showing up in what's called the Heinz 57 effect (a complex blending, as in the "57 Varieties" on which the noted ketchup company rests its fame).

Dog Is in the Details

Certain dog breeds have distinctive physical traits, or bred giveaways. (In AKC-speak, these are called "hallmarks.") Here is a list of common physical traits and the breed that may have been the cause.

Tricolor. Dogs who are black, brown, and white can be part Bernese mountain dog, Saint Bernard, or beagle.

Fall. Long, spiky hair that falls over the face, like a wig, is called a "fall," and it signals Afghan hound heritage.

Ringed tail. Could have Afghan, basenji, or Akita parentage.

Long body, short legs. Basset hound, dachshund, or corgi.

Achondroplastic legs. Legs that are short, turned-out, and dwarfy-looking may be basset hound or corgi.

Black spots. Irregular black spots on a white coat and/or black spots on pink skin underneath means dalmatian.

Ticked coat. A coat that is spotted, not like a dalmatian's, but more like an impressionist painting may be pointer or spaniel.

Redhead. Not many breeds boast this plush feature, so you can narrow a really red, hairy dog down to being part Irish setter, chow chow, or red golden retriever.

Blue tongue. A feature of the chow chow or shar-pei.

facial hair

ticked coat

erect ears

tufted ears

Double-curled tail. An element of chow chow, Shiba Inu, Norwegian elkhound, Akita, keeshond.

Lionlike face and mane (ruff). Chow chow.

Fluffy coat. Chow chow, border collie, poodle.

Long snout, narrow head. Collie, greyhound, Afghan hound.

Wiry coat. Wires mean terrier. They may appear anywhere on the dog, sometimes just in the beard.

Feathered tail. A tail fringed with longish hair is usually seen on retrievers and setters.

Drop ears. Long, rounded "drop" ears indicate the presence of beagle or other hunting-hound genes. Extra-long ears would indicate some basset or bloodhound. Extra-long with fringed tips says spaniel.

Tipped ears. Also called semiprick ears—which are erect with tips that flop forward—suggest collie, border collie, or sheltie.

Erect ears. Shepherd, husky.

Facial hair. Distinctive facial hair—beard, chin whiskers, mustache, eyebrows—means schnauzer, Bouvier, Airedale, or their smaller terrier cousins.

Furnishings. Long hair on the extremities suggests chow chow or border collie.

Brindle. A tiger-striped coat, usually black and brown or tan and gray, is typical of greyhounds, boxers, pit bulls, and mastiffs.

Apron. Long hair under the neck and on the chest, like a cavalier's frilly collar, could indicate border collie or chow chow.

Blue merle. Black marks on a bluish-gray coat suggests collie, Australian cattle dog, or Australian shepherd.

Tufted ears. Ears that stand up with long hair falling from them, like the headdress of a medieval princess, are classic briard.

Brown eyebrows on a black face. Rottweiler.

dalmatian spots

brindle

tipped ears

achondroplastic legs

To Thine Own Mutt Be True

Once you know a little bit more about mutts and the ways their looks can clue you in to their behaviors and needs, sit down and figure out what you know about yourself. When you know mutts and you know yourself, you can determine the type of mutt that's right for you.

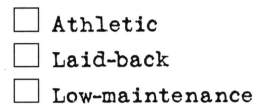

☐ **Athletic**
☐ **Laid-back**
☐ **Low-maintenance**

Are you the athletic type who runs several miles a day? Then definitely look for an athletic, high-energy mutt who will gladly become your jogging partner. Are you more laid-back? Then opt for a more sedate, older mutt. Are you a low-maintenance type whose idea of grooming is a three-minute shower? Then you'll want a mutt with a short, low-maintenance coat as opposed to one who needs daily brushing and frequent grooming. Your lifestyle and your mutt's needs should complement each other, or neither one of you will be happy. Some mutts are more reserved; others are gloriously affectionate, covering your face with kisses. Again, know yourself: Do you mind a dog energetically licking your face and hands? Or would you prefer calmer displays of canine affection?

Contrary to popular belief, the size of your home does not dictate the size of your mutt. As long as the dog gets three or four outings every day to exercise and "do his business," you can easily keep a large mutt in a small apartment (I did). After all, they're not going to get their exercise indoors!

If you have kids pressuring you to adopt a mutt, that's even more reason to know yourself and your family. As the adult, you—not your child—will be responsible for the dog's needs, no matter how much the child promises to care for the dog. Don't ever believe a child who promises to walk and feed the dog "all by myself" (besides, young children should not be entrusted with walking dogs alone, especially at night). With all the pressures of school and after-school activities, it's just not possible for kids to assume the primary care of a dog; rare are the children who don't break all their prepuppy promises. Children have lots to learn from growing up with a mutt, and mutts are wonderful companions who can do wonders to boost kids' self-esteem and positive outlook. But you must realize that the mutt's caretaker will be you. Really think this through: Do you have time in your schedule to add three dog walks to your routine? Realistically, this is what will happen, no matter what your angelic, beseeching child tells you.

FATALE FLAWS

Traits that are deemed unacceptable in a purebred dog are officially known as faults. I think of these flaws not as fatal, but as *fatale*, as in drop-dead gorgeous, and part of what makes a mutt a feast for the eyes.

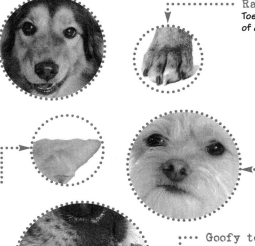

Mask: When two different-colored coats collide, there often results an impressive widow's peak that imparts a great deal of wolverine character to a mutt's countenance.

Rainbow manicure: Toenails (also called horns) of different colors.

Pink nose: In AKC-speak, this is called a "Dudley" nose, and it's considered a "serious fault." Mutt Mavens, on the other hand, think pink noses are seriously cute. So if your adorably faulty mutt has a pink nose, do what a Mutt Maven would do: Apply pet-safe sunscreen (SPF 15) before heading out in the hot sun. One is made by Fauna, an all-natural bath line for pets and people to share.

Nacho-chip ears: Can be pointed or rounded at the tips and as different as one nacho chip is from another. Part of a mutt's survival strategy is knowing how to tilt his head to showcase his asymmetrical ears.

Goofy teeth: Mickey Mouse's pal, like so many mixed breeds, has funny-looking teeth. In dog show parlance, anything less than perfect dentition, whether undershot or overshot, is called "bad mouth." But for Mutt Mavens, bad is good. Underbites, snaggleteeth—these dental quirks are charming.

The Quality of Mercy

by Melissa Holbrook Pierson

Mercy was many things. In the beginning, the tag above her cage read "Lab/Husky Mix," but it could have said "Briard/Dachshund" for all we knew about it, though the truth was closer to "Border Collie/Imp of the Perverse/Astrophysicist." She stepped on top of her brother without concern to get to us, and get to us she did.

She was closed-mouthed about her history. For a while, we felt a compulsion to find out about her parents, what became of her siblings—a sort of reverse adoptive child-parental quest on her behalf. As if we were to somehow "own" her. From her silence as well as that of the SPCA, we were ultimately to learn the message of all such amalgamated creatures that come from cages (*from cages! love and wonderment, from cages!*): "I was not created by you humans. I have my own unfathomable life, as you have yours." It was ultimately to be our tragedy, too, that we could not hold on to her any more than we could stop her from launching herself, a black projectile, toward a prey in flight.

In the beginning, she was thrown away. And her every waking moment as a canine genius was a rebuke to the world that would have done such a thing, that in fact does such things thousands of times a day. "Mercy is a Maserati," was the saying of our first trainer, retained within days of installing this unknown and unknowable puppy in our household, in order to retain our sanity and at least a few of our remaining possessions.

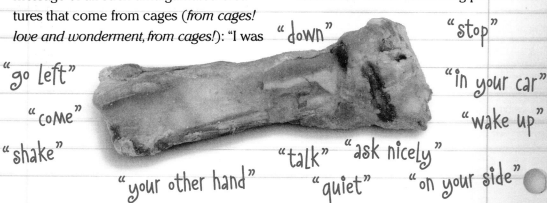

"down" "stop"

"go left" "in your car"

"come" "wake up"

"shake" "talk" "ask nicely"

"your other hand" "quiet" "on your side"

"She is as highly tuned as an exotic sports car, and she's going to take that kind of maintenance and precision driving." Oh, goody. This black-and-white beauty, this well-stirred stew of ancient canine influences, was equal parts curse and blessing. She had a real sense of humor.

Look back ten years. Can you remember when she first figured out that these inscrutable noises coming out of your mouth could actually be fashioned into keys to unlock the treat bin, the holy of all holies? All you recall is that it seemed, suddenly one day, that a transparent window appeared in the side of her head above one floppy ear so you could see a towering complex of gears turning and meshing at all different speeds, perfectly lubricated, small wheels inside of bigger ones. That's when you realized *you* weren't teaching *her* things, it was the other way around, you idiot, and it would ever be thus. She turned you into a reward-dispensing machine, and if she didn't like your particular reward, she was quick to show you what would have worked better, nyah-nyah-nyah. All those things she came to "get," usually with one or at most two repetitions necessary to imprint it in her growing catalog of English-language verbs—circle right, go left, shake, your other hand, talk, quiet, ask nicely, on your side, wake up, in your car, talk, quiet, wait, up on the bed, stop, down, come— you can no longer remember teaching, just that one day you realized you were having conversations *in paragraph form* and she was hearing every word. All you know now, looking backward over what has become a decade reworked by the mechanics of grief, is that it would have been impossible not to love her with an immeasurable completeness of heart, mind, and whatever else you are made of.

> She turned you into a reward-dispensing machine, and if she didn't like your particular reward, she was quick to show you what would have worked better.

She used to laugh at you after she had enjoyed the fruits of one of her more advanced computations in the field of geometry. The opening angle of the triangle was posited by a particularly redolent example of formerly living tissue. The first leg was marked by you, feeling triumphantly clever at having exchanged a treat for "capture" on leash. The second was drawn by both of you, walking away from the estimable treasure in order to leave it forever behind. As the human, of course, your intellect was superior, and so you were certain when the point had been reached that she could be let safely off-leash to continue your bucolic recreation. Indeed, it seemed to be so, as she continued serenely at your side, placating your self-worth by sniffing things, feigning momentary interest in the doings of other dogs. But you had obviously not twigged what was really going on in that lovely brain of hers. Those small glances from large, melting brown eyes were not exactly reassurances of undying fealty

As the human, of course, your intellect was superior... but you were no border collie mix, were you?

and should have tipped you off, but you were no *border collie mix,* were you? She was in fact calculating the exact degree of angle in order to figure length of hypotenuse. Into her mental computer were being fed bits of data, including your rates of walking and running speed, abnormalities of terrain, and size and density of the prize. When the clicking in her brain ceased, she knew the exact spot at which she could stop, stare at you with a look composed equally of pity and glee, and take off like a shot. When you at last arrived panting within five feet of where she lay, the final morsel—no more, no less—would be disappearing down her throat. She would rise and resume her place by your side. *Say, you wouldn't happen to have a napkin, would you?*

Three months, give or take, before what would have been her tenth birthday, she spent the weekend visiting some old stomping grounds, so Monday was a relatively restful day after the excitement of the trip. She had gone on a minor forage with you, down behind the barn, across the overgrown pasture, a little nip into the horse paddock for a fortifying

snack of manure, then a few feints
at the squirrels who were silly
enough to imagine she didn't know
full well she couldn't climb a tree
and wasn't about to bother trying. When
she arose from her post-outing nap, she
suddenly staggered bizarrely, recovered
quickly, and shot you a look that clearly
said *I am scared, because that was finally
one thing I don't understand.* You, in
exactly the same moment, said to yourself, *I am watching my dog die before my
very eyes, and I can't do anything about it.*
This was followed immediately by
another apprehension: *And I won't be
able to survive the sorrow.* In fact,
it would take two weeks for her to
receive the subsequent blows that would
cause her to die, but the other part was
true: You didn't survive, not really.

You went looking everywhere for her.
You began to haunt the animal shelters,
thinking you might turn a corner and
there she would be in her cage, eight
weeks old and throwing herself at the
bars as if to say, *How dare you leave me
here?* Dozens of little pictures of Border
Collie Xs in Your Area appeared daily in
your Internet in-box. You perused them
with the kind of concentration that hurt
your head. There, wait, enlarge this one;

something in
those eyes—maybe
we should go see this
one, because what if it's
her? You patted the head of
every dog you could, so you
could feel her velvet blackness
under your hand once more. You put
out the word that you were looking,
looking. You could still hear her in the
night. Maybe she would just show up on
the doorstep, it was possible, wasn't it,
since everyone kept telling you, "Your
dog will show up when the time is right."
In the meantime, since she would know
that you had not abandoned her, you
had just not found her yet, you put a
name on your wrist with ink that would
last as long as you did: *Mercy.*

The waiting seemed interminable,
but nothing ever is. And so one day
you found yourself driving to Scranton,
Pennsylvania, to look at an eight-week-
old puppy. She had brown eyes. She

metaphorically stepped on top of her brother, whose shyness caused him to fail the behavioral tests even though he won in the handsome category. You cradled her soft whiteness in your hands and said, *Yes*.

History whistled in your ear. You tried to find out from the rescuers who her parents might have been, what had happened to her siblings. Some answers appeared but not all; she was holding her cards close to her chest. You waited for her wiry gray "culottes" of hind-leg hair to appear, the legacy of what may well have been some husky way back in the line (you were certain now no vestige of Lab would ever show up). You tried to remember at what point the tail would fill out into a gorgeously flowing flag.

And then you walked into the wall, because you were looking back and could not see what was solid in front. Nelly was refusing to get bigger; by six months she was only creeping up to the nineteen-pound range, where you kept thinking she *should* have been at least forty by then. Her tail was staying definitively crooked, with no plume in sight. She did strange things that jolted you, because they had not happened before: She buried her bones (in the bedclothes or potted palm, if necessary) instead of wolfing them immediately. She preferred digging in dirt to chasing things like a maniac. She refused to become anyone but Nelly.

Through the vague disappointment you feel, you see her in the distance, shining a light, waving a paw. *Hey, over here! Follow me, out from that sad place!* If you look forward toward where she is—yes, laughing a little!—you will see that she is giving you an opportunity. As do all of her kind, which are like no other kind. Her mother might have been a border collie, but her daddy is a lingering mystery running through her DNA. Jack Russell? Papillon? Or self-owned mongrel himself? The opportunity is to stop worrying about that—about the past. She is here before you in her insular glory. Like all her mut-tish kin, she is a one-off. There is some lesson in that, but she cautions you not to look so hard at it, either. *(Hey, isn't that a terrier thing?)* Nelly will be her resolute, small, white self. Mercy, in her unrepeatable way, has come back again.

The Breed Trait List

Here is a recap of the most popular purebred dogs and the traits they exhibit. If you look for mixes of the breeds you like, you'll find that you usually get a nice, subdued variation of the purebred qualities.

RETRIEVERS ....▶ *easygoing, athletic, large*

GERMAN SHEPHERDS ....▶ *large, muscular, intelligent, workers*

CORGIS ....▶ *small, herders, determined*

POODLES ....▶ *intelligent, eager to please, soft-coated*

BASSET HOUNDS ....▶ *laid-back, couch potatoes, heavier than they look*

BEAGLES ....▶ *like to bay, hunters, friendly*

PUGS ....▶ *lapdogs, nonathletic, prone to be overweight*

CHIHUAHUAS ....▶ *feisty, watchdogs, prefer adults*

DALMATIANS ....▶ *love running, endurance athletes*

PIT BULLS/BOXERS ....▶ *affectionate, outgoing, very strong*

BOSTON TERRIERS ....▶ *lapdogs, prefer adults, feisty*

BULLDOGS ....▶ *couch potatoes, dislike heat*

DACHSHUNDS ....▶ *snugglers, prone to back problems*

COLLIES ....▶ *herders, love to run, easygoing*

CHOW CHOW ....▶ *protective, get attached to owners*

Every family has its
genealogical tree.
The family of Mutt is no exception.
Here are the types of
canine mixes you're most likely
to encounter.

The Mutt
Family Tree

The German shepherd mix is one of the most common dogs in America. Mutt fanciers believe that the beauty of purebred shepherds is only enhanced by the introduction of traits from other breeds. Shepherd mixes come in an enormous variety of shapes; their coats may be thicker or thinner than the purebred shepherd, their bodies wider or more slender, but their shepherd identity remains strong. Like their unmixed counterparts, shepherd mixes are dedicated workers—and intelligent enough to perform even challenging tasks.

shepherd & greyhound mix

LADDIE

The extra-long snout, large nose, and close-set eyes suggest that this shepherd mix is part greyhound (check out those long, skinny legs) or collie.

shepherd

greyhound

shepherd & collie mix

shepherd

collie

The characteristic shepherd marking—black shadings on tan ground—assert themselves in Kimber's lovely coat. Her serious expression and ever-ready stance are also characteristic of the hardworking shepherd.

SCRIBBLE

Scribble's plush tail and reddish coat suggest that he is part border collie. His sweet face is enhanced by a black mask.

KIMBER

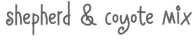

shepherd & coyote mix

Down South, there's a certain type of shepherd-coyote mix known as a Carolina dog or American dingo. Cassidy is a fine example; note her extra-thick, black-tipped tail, which appears to be borrowed from a raccoon.

CASSIDY

coyote

shepherd

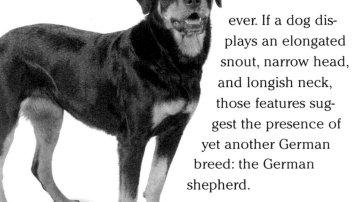

Large size and distinctive black-and-tan markings are bred giveaways that a mutt is part rottweiler, a German breed developed for guarding and cattle-herding duty. Mixes usually don't have the rottie's massive head, however. If a dog displays an elongated snout, narrow head, and longish neck, those features suggest the presence of yet another German breed: the German shepherd.

rottweiler & shepherd mix

Baby has a regal, long snout that's pure shepherd (unlike the boxy rottie snout), but she has the rottie's short, glossy coat.

Ears are longer and narrower than a rottweiler's—shaped like shepherd ears, but they hang down rather than stand erect.

Rust eyebrows are a classic rottweiler feature.

german shepherd

rottweiler

BABY

rottweiler & shepherd mix

Whereas a pure rottweiler is predominantly black (according to the AKC breed standard, "Rust markings should not exceed 10 percent of body color"), Maximus has rust all over, and his shepherd traits predominate.

Tan eyebrows, cheeks, and throat rott-ify this otherwise classically shepherd face.

MAXIMUS

rottweiler & shepherd mix

ROCCO

rottweiler

On Rocco's coat, the combined black-and-tan coloring of the shepherd predominates; he also has a triangle of white fur on his chest, which neither breed is supposed to have—that's a *fatale* flaw (one that disqualifies a dog from the show ring but endears him to a Mutt Maven).

shepherd

rottweiler & bernese mountain dog mix

Mongo has a much thicker, furrier coat than the short-coated rottweiler, giving him the plush, winterized appearance of a Bernese mountain dog.

bernese mountain dog

rottweiler

MONGO

When terriers mingle with other breeds, they can be leggy and tall or short and small, but they always retain the whiskery look of their terrier heritage, complete with beard, mustache, and feathered ears.

wheaten
terrier

west highland
white terrier
(a.k.a. westie)

cairn
terrier

norwich
terrier

westie-wheaten-norwich terrier mix

A summit of terriers convenes in the aptly named Terry, who displays traits of the cairn, Westie, wheaten, and Norwich terriers. Her shaggy coat is at once wiry and soft to the touch; it would be scruffy, but it's clipped short.

TERRY

westie

norwich terrier

wheaten terrier

terrier & lab mix

Lola has the body size and type of a Lab; with her wiry blond coat, she resembles a tall wheaten terrier. Her willingness to work and her strong resemblance to Sandy, the canine sidekick of Little Orphan Annie, has led her to be cast as Sandy in productions of the musical *Annie*.

wheaten terrier

lab

LOLA

terrier & chihuahua mix

Pancho is small enough to indicate that his ancestry incorporates the tiny Chihuahua (his slender muzzle is also Chihuahualike), hence his Mexican name. The wiry frills in his coat, however, reveal the infusion of Anglo blood from terrier ancestors.

PANCHO

westie

chihuahua

terrier & schnauzer mix

schnauzer

westie

Sadie's charcoal-gray coat with white markings indicates she's a substantial part schnauzer, a type of terrier; one of her ears is erect, like a schnauzer's, while the other flops down (asymmetrical ears being a mutt trademark). Her playful attitude fairly defines "bright-eyed and bushy-tailed," with her forelegs wide apart in a perpetual play-bow and her tail tirelessly wagging.

SADIE

boston terrier & shih tzu mix

When a Boston terrier hooked up with a shih tzu (a toy breed originally from China), the result was Fred, who has the shih tzu's soft, long hair (Fred's is clipped short), but in the brindle-and-white pattern characteristic of the short-coated Boston.

boston terrier

shih tzu

FRED

A white-tipped tail *is always a handsome distinguishing feature in any mutt.*

Both of the breeds *that went into this mix share a pushed-in face.*

Note the muscular legs *and fearless stance of the Boston terrier.*

A white bib *gives the aristocratic air of formalwear.*

DALMATIAN MIX

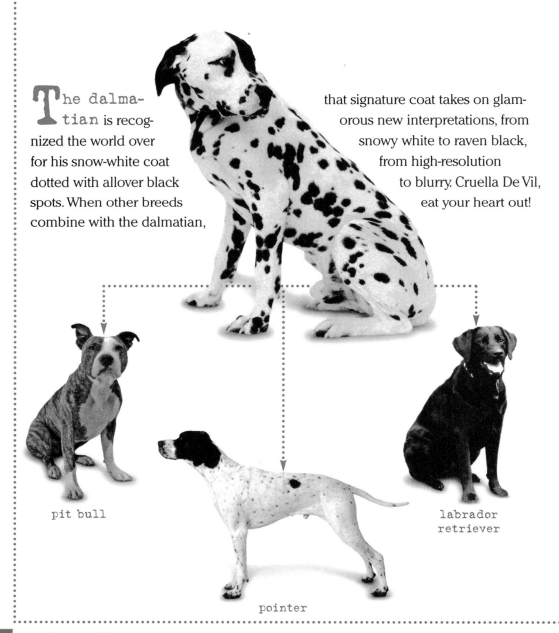

The dalmatian is recognized the world over for his snow-white coat dotted with allover black spots. When other breeds combine with the dalmatian, that signature coat takes on glamorous new interpretations, from snowy white to raven black, from high-resolution to blurry. Cruella De Vil, eat your heart out!

pit bull

pointer

labrador retriever

dalmatian & pit bull mix

Lily has the muscular physique, wide head, and soulful expression of a pit bull, with faded dalmatian spots on her body and legs. The spots show up darker on her ears, with the darkest one over her left eye—as if a celebrity makeup artist piled on eyeliner to make this beauty look like Petey, the Little Rascals' mascot.

LILY

adopt me!

BIGGY

dalmatian & black lab mix

Reversing the equation is Biggy, a dalmatian noir who's part black Lab. However, his head and ears are perfectly dalmatian, and he wears perfect, high-resolution, dalmatian-spotted socks on all four feet.

dalmatian & pointer mix

Greta, a dalmatian-pointer mix, is generously dotted all over her body, with dalmatianlike spots and pointerlike ticking, plus black ears and distinctively large, black spots inked over both eyes.

GRETA

The border collie, a sheepherding breed originating in the region bordering Scotland and England, is most often seen wearing a thick, black-and-white double coat like Lucy's. Sometimes, however, they come with glorious sable hair like Sheba's. The lighter red hair on her legs and underbelly suggests the presence in her ancestry of a redhead breed such as Irish setter. The ticking on Lucy's coat, on the other hand, suggests spaniel heritage.

The close-set eyes, designed to enable the border collie to control sheep with an intense stare called "the eye," give an alert, intelligent expression. "Furnishings" on the hind legs give the impression of pantaloons.

chow chow

spaniel

border collie & chow chow mix

··· **An undershot bite** is a "serious flaw" in a purebred border collie; Sheba's lower jaw juts out a full inch past her upper, resulting in an endearing *fatale* flaw. Her coat is as fuzzy as a chow's and as red as an Irish setter's.

SHEBA

border collie & spaniel mix

··· **Paws** generously covered with hair between the toes are a border collie or spaniel trait, but Lucy's are exceptionally hirsute. Another sign that Lucy is part spaniel: her smaller size and feathery ears.

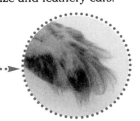

LUCY

The greyhound's sleek physique features a wasp waist. When mixed, the fleet-footed long-distance runner of the dog world takes on other traits, but his greyhound heritage is hard to overlook. Greyhound mixes, like pure greyhounds, are as adept at sofa-lounging as they are at running.

lab

collie

pit bull

greyhound & Lab mix

CHUKKER

Chukker is almost 99 percent pure, with classic black-and-white greyhound markings, a large, tall, elegant physique, and a bit of Lab thrown in to fill him out and give him a slightly broader muzzle, thicker neck, and more rugged silhouette overall. Chukker assumes very regal, sphinxlike postures characteristic of the noble greyhound.

greyhound & collie mix

IGOR

Igor's ready-for-his-closeup smile is pure Lassie, indicating he's part collie. But unlike Lassie, his coat is smooth and short. His tricolor (black, brown, and white) coat is characteristic of a collie. Both the collie and greyhound share a long, slender muzzle and close-set eyes. Igor's face is split down the middle, half white and half brown, for a distinctive "two-faced" effect.

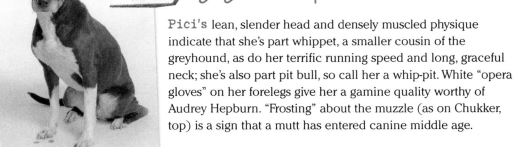

PICI

greyhound & pit bull mix

Pici's lean, slender head and densely muscled physique indicate that she's part whippet, a smaller cousin of the greyhound, as do her terrific running speed and long, graceful neck; she's also part pit bull, so call her a whip-pit. White "opera gloves" on her forelegs give her a gamine quality worthy of Audrey Hepburn. "Frosting" about the muzzle (as on Chukker, top) is a sign that a mutt has entered canine middle age.

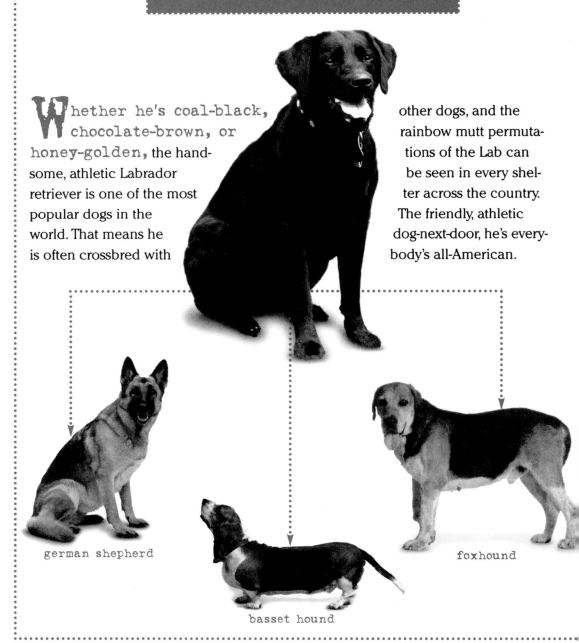

Whether he's coal-black, chocolate-brown, or honey-golden, the handsome, athletic Labrador retriever is one of the most popular dogs in the world. That means he is often crossbred with other dogs, and the rainbow mutt permutations of the Lab can be seen in every shelter across the country. The friendly, athletic dog-next-door, he's everybody's all-American.

german shepherd

basset hound

foxhound

Lab retriever & german shepherd mix

Elsie's blond coat color and light eyes give her a golden appearance. But her muzzle, ending in a pink "Dudley" nose, is narrower than that of a Lab, suggesting the presence of German shepherd in her mutt makeup.

ELSIE

Lab retriever & basset hound mix

OLIVER

Oliver's coat, head, and bushy tail are those of the yellow Lab; the elongated body and dwarfy, turned-out achondroplastic legs are those of the basset hound.

Lab retriever & foxhound mix

DUDLEY

Wearing the glossy raven coat and upbeat expression of the black Lab, Dudley also has the hound's adorably droopy face, low-hung ears, and deep, fleshy flews (the pendulous lateral part of the upper lip). His white bib and white-tipped paws give him a dashing black-tie appearance. Black "ticking" (patterns of small spots) on the coat is a hound trait; here the ticking is concentrated on the throat and chest. Further intriguing contrast is provided by the white blaze, or stripe, running the length of his snout all the way to the top of his head.

A word about poodles: They are mercilessly made fun of, but their reputation as froufrou circus performers is not their fault. Poodles' high IQ and willingness to please mean they've always been quick studies when it comes to learning complicated tricks. This character trait has been exploited for centuries by circus and carnival folk, who made spectacles out of their performing poodles by dressing them in tutus and making them dance on their hind legs or turn somersaults. Free of stereotypical poodle trappings, hybridized with other types of dog (most commonly terriers) so their soft, delicate hair assumes a rougher texture, poodle mixes take on a different, more *sportif* attitude.

miniature
poodle

standard poodle

poodle & terrier mix

poodle

westie

The **expressive eyes,** button nose, and elongated snout are those of the poodle. A terrier's ears usually stand erect; a poodle has drop ears. The poodle mix's ears find a middle ground, often managing to go horizontal.

DILSEY

poodle & yorkshire terrier mix

A **poodle-Yorkshire terrier** hybrid, Holly has an impressive prancing gait.

HOLLY

yorkshire terrier

poodle

poodle & chihuahua mix

chihuahua

miniature poodle

The **whitish hair** has highlights of the palest apricot—a classic poodle coat color. The poodle mix's long limbs permit a prancing gait and give Nora a leg up when assuming dainty, wristy poses.

NORA

S mall dogs with small heads, smooth coats, and something extra— say, a somewhat larger and/or longer body than the average Chihuahua—these endearing little mixes tend to be hardier than their purebred cousins, who often shiver even when it's not that cold out. A Chihuahua mix is still toy size, but he's a lot of dog in a compact package and demands to be taken seriously. When a mutt combines Chihuahua and terrier, rodents had better run for cover—that's double the ratting instinct in one dog.

chihuahua & pug mix

chihuahua

pug

Asymmetrical ears, besides being indescribably cute, are a sure sign that a dog is a mix of two or more breeds— in this case, two very popular toy breeds, the Chihuahua and the pug. That tightly curled tail is the sure sign that a pug figures prominently in this dog's ancestry.

DUMPLING

chihuahua & wirehaired terrier mix

ELLIE

chihuahua

wirehaired terrier

Note the Mohawk of wiry hair down Ellie's back, giving her the Jurassic profile of *Triceratops*—an effect easily enhanced by back-combing the hairs from tail to neck!

chihuahua & spaniel mix

chihuahua

RUSTINO

His feathery ears and tail indicate that Rusty is part spaniel, as do his smooth, silky coat and *sportif* demeanor.

spaniel

chihuahua & jack russell mix

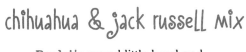

chihuahua

Pooki's round little head and wide-eyed expression are textbook Chihuahua, as are her dainty legs, the front paws turned out ballerina-style. Her legs, tail, and body resemble those of a stouter breed: the Jack Russell terrier.

jack russell

POOKI

chihuahua & shepherd mix

chihuahua

shepherd

Bark like an Egyptian: These mutts have a regal bearing worthy of artifacts in King Tut's tomb in common. Preston and Sydney are both fine examples of a mixed breed having the beauty of a purebred: They resemble miniaturized versions of a pedigreed Pharaoh Hound.

. . . whereas Sydney's ears are larger and more shepherdlike.

Preston is a small mutt, perhaps a Chihuahua with some larger breed such as German shepherd in his ancestry.

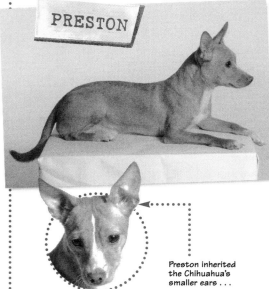

PRESTON

SYDNEY

Preston inherited the Chihuahua's smaller ears . . .

Sydney reverses the equation, being a very petite shepherd mix. Both have heads resembling Anubis, the Egyptian jackal deity, and are adept at striking regal, sphinxlike poses.

GOLDEN RETRIEVER MIX

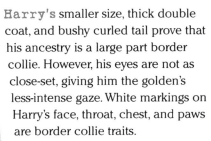

The golden retriever consistently ranks as one of the country's top three favorite dog breeds. It's no wonder, then, that permutations of this blond bombshell turn up with such frequency at shelters—and they're even more stunning than ordinary goldens, because they're more unusual.

golden retriever & chow chow mix

chow chow

golden retriever

Manny displays the golden's rich, silky coat and brush tail, enhanced by the blue-black tongue of the chow chow, as well as the chow chow's plush ruff of double-thick fur about the neck and chest.

MANNY

golden retriever & border collie mix

Harry's smaller size, thick double coat, and bushy curled tail prove that his ancestry is a large part border collie. However, his eyes are not as close-set, giving him the golden's less-intense gaze. White markings on Harry's face, throat, chest, and paws are border collie traits.

border collie

golden retriever

HARRY

Animal shelters, especially those in or within a few miles of urban areas, have more pit bulls and pit mixes than loving homes to adopt them due to widespread fear of pits. Yet many of the most beautiful, lovable, and eligible mutts are predominantly pit. The mixes take many different forms, but the characteristic muscular physique, wide head, and big heart always come across in translation.

pit bull & rhodesian ridgeback mix

pit bull

rhodesian ridgeback

Canyon's predominantly tan coat; long, rounded ears; and soulful, black-rimmed eyes are those of a Rhodesian ridgeback, the large hound known for having a dorsal "zipper" of against-the-grain fur.

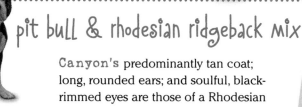

CANYON

pit bull & yellow lab mix

Her yellow Lab roots are evident in Cashmere's thick, luxurious blond coat. She's also taller and less muscular than a straight pit bull, with a narrower chest and deep, Labby flews (the folds of skin over the upper jaw).

yellow lab

CASHMERE

The pit-ness is in the angular profile.

pit bull

pit bull & basset hound mix

VASCO

That Vasco is part basset hound is evident in his elongated body and short, dwarfy legs. The musculature is sheer pit.

pit bull

Vasco's tail mark matches his facial mask.

basset hound

These mutts combine the pit bull's athletic build with a narrower head and chest; larger, floppier ears; and tan or brown markings. Their smooth coats and can-do attitudes make them equally at home in the country and the city.

pit bull & foxhound mix

This is a very winning mix that's quite common in the American South.

Note Edie's curled, bushy tail, a hound characteristic (pit bulls have thin, short-coated tails).

EDIE

pit bull

foxhound

pit bull & pointer mix

Wrigley sports the head of a pointer and a perfect beauty spot in the middle of his back (being a mutt, he's smart enough to strike a pose to show the spot off to advantage). His square muzzle reveals his pit parentage.

WRIGLEY

pit bull

pointer

pit bull & boxer mix

The boxer and pit bull share a strong, muscular physique.

pit bull

boxer

HONEY

Honey has the tricolor (fawn, white, and black) markings of a boxer, but instead of the boxer's pushed-in face, blunt, upturned muzzle, and underbite, he has the enlongated muzzle and wide, rounded forehead of a pit bull. A black mask stretching from eyes to cheeks is offset by a wide white blaze running the length of the snout. A black "paw-di-cure" is shown to advantage against white "socks." A black beauty mark on each cheek adds further distinction to a very distinguished face.

ROCKY

With Rocky, the broad muzzle and wide head mean the emphasis is on the pit bull part of his ancestry.

The sad, soulful expression is classic pit.

shepherd

pit bull

pit bull & shepherd mix

This is a very common hybrid at animal shelters across the United States.

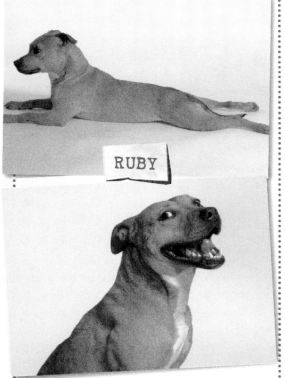

RUBY

Ruby displays subtle shepherdlike black shading on her tan coat, a white bib, and the irresistible grin for which pit bulls are known, as well as the pits' endearing habit of stretching their hind legs straight out behind them while lying down, like frogs.

RUSTY

With his black tiger stripes on brown, Rusty demonstrates the classic "brindle" pattern often seen on pits.

A blend of two dogs built for the hunt, Lola has the head, Snoopy ears, and medium-size body type of a beagle, but she's leggy like a pointer, with the pointer's ticked coat and graphic spots. That heritage gives her twice the hunting drive; no rabbit is safe around her! Black and white are combined artfully in Lola's coat, with her mostly black head balancing her heavily spotted rear end and paws dipped lightly in black.

beagle

pointer

LOLA

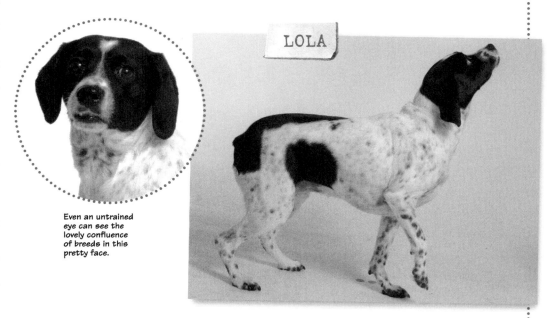

Even an untrained eye can see the lovely confluence of breeds in this pretty face.

The chow chow is an ancient Chinese breed set apart by his plush double coat, blue-black tongue, and double-curled tail. He takes on even more distinctive features when blended with other breeds.

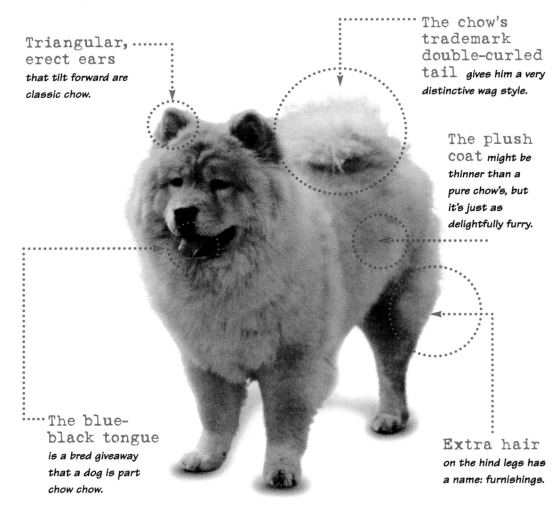

Triangular, erect ears *that tilt forward are classic chow.*

The chow's trademark double-curled tail *gives him a very distinctive wag style.*

The plush coat *might be thinner than a pure chow's, but it's just as delightfully furry.*

The blue-black tongue *is a bred giveaway that a dog is part chow chow.*

Extra hair *on the hind legs has a name: furnishings.*

chow chow & shepherd mix

chow chow

shepherd

AMBER

Madison's hair is kept short; she has unusual ears with dark tufts of hair that arc outward and down, giving her the impression of having a perm. Her tongue, while not entirely blue-black, has large, dark spots.

Amber's long, black muzzle and black markings about the head are signs that she is part German shepherd. Her coat is also shorter than a chow chow's, with a texture closer to that of the shepherd.

MADISON

TAYLOR

chow chow & briard mix

chow chow

Taylor has the blue-black tongue of the chow chow, but the French herding breed known as the briard played a major role in his background, as evidenced by his signature upright ears, accented by long, glorious tufts of hair, and his muzzle, which is narrower than that of a chow chow.

briard

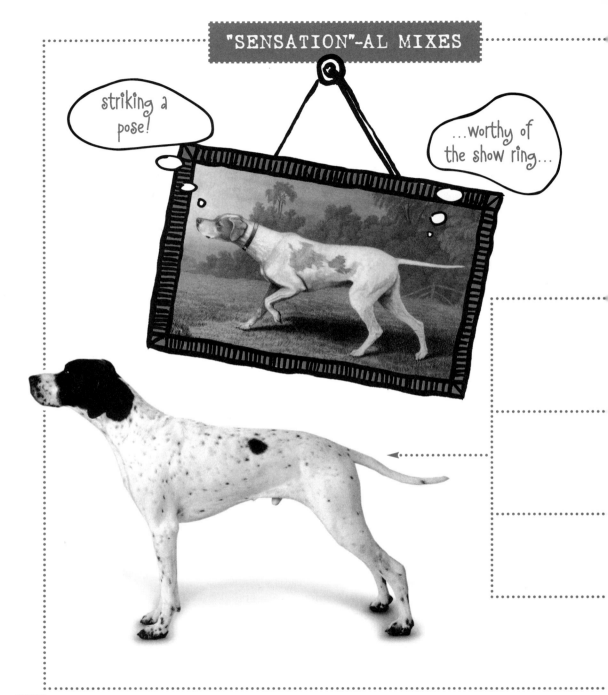

A famous nineteenth-century pointer named "Sensation" will live on forever as the emblem of the Westminster Kennel Club Dog Show. He's depicted in profile, hunting down quarry, to show off his perfect conformation. Need visual proof that mixed breeds also possess a proud, noble bearing and deserve appreciation, too? Look no further than these "sensation"-al mutts.

. . . even the nonpointers point. . .

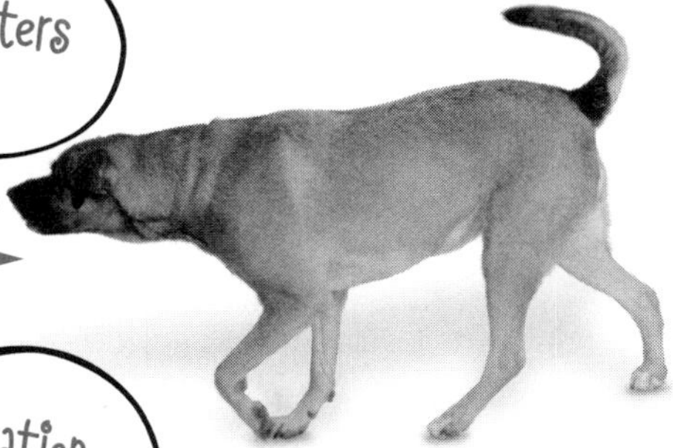

. . . we mutts are ready for our close-up. . .

Sensation, eat your heart out!

shepherd mix

heinz 57

border collie mix

pointer-lab mix

99 percent pure

Mostly Husky: Jesse The body shape, erect ears, and—most important—blue eyes are bred giveaways of Jesse's husky heritage. His coat has the plush, dense texture of a dog suited for Arctic climates, but it's a single coat (as opposed to the double coat of the purebred husky).

Mostly Maltese: Happy-Go-Lucky Happy is a fine example of a mixed breed that's "99 percent pure"—almost all one breed, but with a butch twist. Predominantly Maltese, the toy dog known for his long, silky, white coat, Happy has a more substantial head than most Malteses and wears the silky white coat on a stouter body. The hair is clipped short (as a rule, mutts don't need to spend nearly as much time at the groomer's as their purebred counterparts). Note the absence of ribbons and bows (a point of mutt pride).

Mostly Shar-pei: Margie She has the unmistakable face, black "hippopotamus" muzzle, and tan coat of the

are you a mutt?

Jesse

Me too!

Who's that dog?

Happy-Go-Lucky!

ancient Chinese breed, without the loose, folded skin that causes many shar-peis to have health problems. Her other main ingredient appears to be pit bull, to judge by her muscular body shape and short coat. (Both shar-peis and pit bulls have wrinkly foreheads, the latter having many fewer wrinkles.)

Mostly Beagle: Maya Maya has the signature long Snoopy ears and short, compact build of this fearless hunting dog, but she's smaller of body and narrower of head. Her coat is typical beagle tricolor, but the areas of white are more prominent. The real sign, however, that she's not all beagle is auditory, not visual. Maya's only been heard to bay twice in three years (the average beagle lets out a rallying cry a lot more often than that).

impure and proud!

What a profile!

Maya has a flyaway ear . . .

Margie smiles.

. . . yet she's very regal.

Mostly Yorkie: Marky

This mutt displays most of the characteristics of the Yorkshire terrier, but he's unusually leggy, suggesting he's mixed with a taller breed.

Mostly Shih Tzu: Minnie

Taller than the average shih tzu but with the facial features characteristic of the

The 99-percenters are just one detail shy of purebred perfection— but it's their imperfections that make them lovable mutts.

Marky speaks.

Marky's lips are sealed.

Minnie - side view

Minnie - curious/confused

everbody thinks i'm cute!

ancient Chinese breed, Minnie's height and larger, more substantial size suggest she's mixed with a slightly bigger breed, such as a terrier.

Mostly Pomeranian: Priscilla

Priscilla is larger than a Pomeranian, with a predominantly black coat, yet everything else, from her prick ears to her bright eyes and bushy, curled tail, says Pom.

Mostly Pekingese: Nina

Don't let the lapdog genes fool you: Peke mixes are hardy survivors (especially if they've got *fatale* flaws like this little gal's too-long snout and undershot bite). In a classic tale of mutt triumph, a Peke mix in Montana made headlines recently after he survived being snatched by an eagle, then endured being lost outdoors in subfreezing temperatures before finding his way home.

i belong on a pedestal . . .

Priscilla

Priscilla - gorgeous from any angle

My coy Minnie

don't you think?

Nina - all tongue

The Attention-getting Heinz 57

So well blended are the ingredients of Billie's mutt makeup that even her adoring guardian is at a loss for what this dog's main components might be—and she's a dog expert. Your guess is as good as anyone's: The wide head and snout, substantial paws, and small-to-medium body size suggest English bulldog; the wiry coat is pure terrier; the eyes indicate the possibility a husky might have entered the mix somewhere (although nothing else about her resembles a husky); and the eagerness to respond to the command "sit pretty" by assuming photogenic postures worthy of a tutu-wearing ballerina has poodle written all over it.

Blue eyes *are a disqualification for most purebreds, but they're not uncommon in white dogs of random breeding (some mutts have one blue eye and one brown eye).*

Light brown patches *on her white coat are artfully arranged, with one covering her left ear.*

The underbite *is one more clue to her possible bulldog ancestry.*

The chin whiskers *appear borrowed from another species, possibly the catfish.*

BILLIE

The "Invisible" Heinz 57

A combination of several canine components—including German shepherd, pit bull, and hound—Maggie is the embodiment of the nondescript mutt. Her many shades of brown— like those of so many mixed breeds—camouflage her in many different environments, challenging a person who values substance over style to take a chance on a plain, brown dog.

Just as blond highlights warm up brunette hair, the white hair on Maggie's throat and chest offers visual intrigue.

A black mask combines with dark eyebrows to give the appearance of Bette Davis, in plain-Jane premakeover mode, from the movie Now Voyager.

Wide-set eyes yield a wise and profoundly soulful expression.

MAGGIE

The Classic Scruffy

Equal parts prince, pauper, and clown, the combination of terrier and shepherd is an unmistakably charming one. Although still just a baby, Bird displays the classic components of a scruffy stray.

His wiry coat is a terrier trait, as are his beard and mustache. The dusky color of the coat suggests the terrier he's mixed with could be a schnauzer; upon further examination, the coat is a brownish-black mélange that resembles the coloring of a German shepherd.

adopt me!

The ears are erect, which is a trait shared by shepherds as well as certain terriers (notably schnauzers).

Bird's long legs suggest he'll grow to be a tall young man—closer in height to a shepherd than a terrier.

BIRD

Physically Challenged Mutts

What others perceive as a physical handicap doesn't cramp a mutt's style. With unbreakable, optimistic spirit, mixed breeds learn to adapt to obstacles so easily, quickly, and cheerfully that you'd have to look hard to notice there's anything different about them.

A "Heinz 57" of shepherd-rottweiler-pit bull, Tiny Tim is so named because his right foreleg was amputated on Christmas Eve after a car accident. He's adapted so well to being a tripod that observers only notice the missing limb after a double take.

Another example of mixed-breed survival, a shepherd-Lab named Winks was born with a defective left eye. The eye had to be surgically removed, but that doesn't stop her from maintaining a happy outlook (check out her cheery smile).

TINY TIM

adopt me!

WINKS

In the nineteenth century,

an Augustinian monk named Gregor Mendel, the father of modern genetics, proved with garden pea-plant experiments that crossbreeding produces healthier, stronger plants than those that are inbred. Not surprisingly, the concept of "hybrid vigor" applies just as well to mixed-breed dogs. Mutts are notorious for having healthy constitutions, often despite having endured less-than-ideal upbringings. It is their astonishing hardiness that has enabled mutts to survive all the indignities that history has heaped on them. Take it from vet Rebecca Campbell, who's seen her fair share of healthy and not-so-healthy dogs:

"The more Heinz 57 mutts are, the healthier they are."

hile purebreds encounter serious health problems due to overbreeding—ailments can range from allergies to hip dysplasia to a propensity to spinal damage—mutts are not characterized by extremes of body size or conformation that become difficult for certain purebred dogs to sustain over time.

> "We have no interest in purebred dogs--we've always had mutts. They're smarter, have fewer medical problems, and they live longer!"

Kevin Bacon and Kyra Sedgwick with Paulie.

As a result, mutts tend to be the hardiest dogs, most leading long lives free of troublesome health issues. That means fewer high-ticket vet bills in the long run, and less heartache worrying over a sickly dog whose problems cannot be cured because he was inbred.

From his various experiments, Gregor Mendel concluded that hereditary factors do not combine, but are passed on intact; that each member of the parental generation transmits only half of its hereditary factors to each offspring; and that different offspring of the same parents receive different sets of hereditary factors. The average mutt litter attests to Mendel's findings, each puppy displaying various distinct parental traits. But the more crossbred a mutt is, the more hybrid vigor that mutt will have to carry him through life problem-free.

Your Mutt, His Health

There are several things to consider when evaluating your mutt's health. The most important are breed, age, condition, and history. The more you know—or intuit—about your mixed-breed companion, the better his chances of enjoying a long and comfortable life.

Breed:

There are certain mutts who look an awful lot like purebreds; as we saw in chapter 3, these are the 99 percent pures (page 106). There's a simple rule of thumb when it comes to these mixed breeds' health: The more a mutt looks like a purebred, the 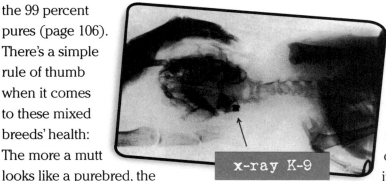 more prone he'll be to health issues that afflict that particular breed. For instance, large dogs like Great Danes, borzois, German shepherds, or greyhounds have a deep-chested conformation that puts them at greater risk for bloat, so take care when feeding them to let them rest at

x-ray K-9

least two hours before exercising. Great Danes and boxers are prone to cardiomyopathy, a life-threatening disease of the heart muscle that can be treated, but not cured. Any mutt that looks a lot like a Great Dane or a boxer can also be expected to have an increased risk for this condition. A mutt resembling a rottweiler or Lab could have inherited hip dysplasia, an orthopedic deformity common to those breeds, that, if severe, can be corrected through expensive hip-replacement surgery. Dogs with long backs, such as dachshunds, corgis, basset hounds, or mixes thereof, are prone to back problems. Another basset trait is dwarfy,

What sort of person adopts the sickliest pup in the animal shelter?

Jeff Hephner. When the star of Fox TV's The Jury saw a scrawny beagle-hound mix, he didn't stop to deliberate; he adopted her and named her Betty. The tiny mutt weighed just five pounds and was in very bad shape. Like a diagram in a veterinary textbook illustrating as many maladies as could possibly befall one animal, the pup displayed several classic baby-mutt ailments. "She was part of an abandoned litter someone found," Hephner recalls. "She was definitely the runt." Like many abandoned pups, Betty suffered from several medical problems at once, including an upper-respiratory infection, intestinal parasites, and rickets. But she also had parvovirus, which is often fatal in pups, making an animal shelter a high-risk environment for very young dogs whose still-developing immune systems have trouble

fighting off the virus. The virus causes vomiting and diarrhea, which spells extra cleanup work. So why did Hephner choose to adopt the saddest, most high-maintenance puppy? "Because she was also the cutest puppy," he explains with a smile. "Plus the fact that nobody else wanted to take her: I took the one that had the longest shot." Adopting any dog is a commitment. But caring for a helpless pup is a major challenge. "We had to feed her with an eyedropper, and she was on a schedule of four different kinds of medication," Hephner says. "For the first month, she kept us up all night." All the effort was well worth it, Hephner reports. "You get so much extra love," he says, cuddling Betty, who now weighs in at her ideal weight, a healthy twenty-three pounds.

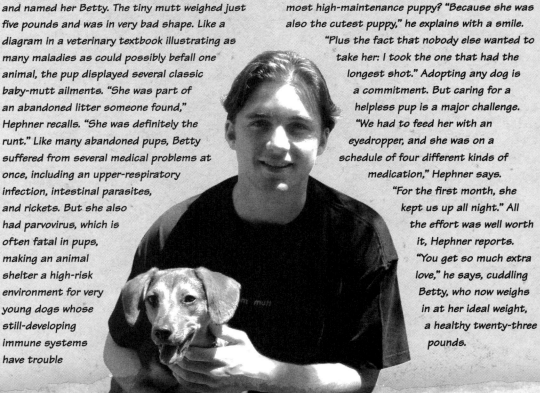

Actor Jeff Hephner with Betty, the mutt pup he adopted and nursed back to health.

turned-out achondroplastic limbs, a deformity of the legs that the dog is intentionally bred for. While certainly cute, those legs can develop significant joint problems from uneven weight distribution and, ultimately, early-onset arthritis. Knowing what medical problems your dog may be inherently prone to will give you a head start on solving them.

Age:

Old dogs experience many of the same symptoms of age that older people do. Their bones become brittle, their joints stiffen, their digestion slows, and they get gray hairs on their snouts (which is called "frosting"). They may develop cataracts, and their hearing may weaken. If they live long enough, they may develop serious illnesses like cancer or diabetes. Your vet will take a guess at your mutt's age by looking at her overall condition and checking her teeth. Caring for an aging mutt is not so different from caring for a young one. The animal should get all the same vaccinations,

About how old is he?

Is she good with kids?

but should see the doctor twice a year for a physical instead of once. Like their human counterparts, senior mutts should stick with a healthy diet and avoid rich foods. They are likely to require glucosamine supplements to support their aging joints.

Condition:

Is your mutt obese? Or is she skin and bones? Does she have a broken bone that was never repaired properly? Does she have parasites—fleas, ticks, or worms—that haven't been treated? Did she pick up kennel cough at the shelter? Have your mutt carefully inspected to be sure you'll know what kind of physical condition she's in and how to address problems. Realize that many ailments are highly treatable. Bacteria, parasites, and coughs are treated with medication. Broken bones are set. Some other conditions can be fixed with simple surgeries or nonsurgical interventions. Even more serious structural conditions like a missing leg or paralysis can be worked around with patience and tolerance.

Does she need to go on a diet?

History:

It's helpful to know as much as you can about your mutt's history, as it can aid in treating her. For example, if she's overweight, is it because she was fed table scraps all her life or because she was spayed late in life? If the former, watching her diet may be enough to slim her down. If the latter, there may be little you can do. Was the dog a stray? Was she loved by a good family? Was she abused by someone cruel? A dog's past may explain some of her behavior and her physical conditions.

Shelter:

A mutt's medical condition may also be determined by which kind of shelter he was in. At kill shelters, where there is a high turnover and little time to pamper, mutts usually exhibit the same health problems as strays. They will be very dirty and quite skinny, and might have parasites. These conditions are all easily fixed, and after a couple of weeks in your care, with low stress, proper nutrition, medication, and thorough grooming, your mutt will be sporting a glossy coat and generally radiant aura. At no-kill shelters, where there is more time to attend to mutts' physical problems and keep abreast of any issues that may arise while the animal is in residence, the dogs are usually in much better shape. Realtors describe an apartment or home as being in "move-in condition"; that's the shape mutts from no-kill shelters are likely to be in. Mutts from kill shelters are often fixer-uppers.

I WILL SURVIVE PHOTO EXCLUSIV

Dosha is a Sanskrit word meaning "force." In Ayurvedic medicine, the doshas are bodily energies. By proving she possessed life force in spades, a pit bull mix named Dosha neatly lived up to her name in 2003, when she cheated death three times in one day. First, she was hit by a truck near her home in Clear Lake, California. A police officer, thinking he was putting her out of pain, attempted emergency field euthanasia by shooting her in the head. Her body was taken to Animal Control, zipped into an orange plastic bag, and placed in a freezer. About two hours later, Dosha was found sitting upright, quite alive. She had a bullet lodged in her skull and was shivering from hypothermia but, amazingly, suffered no broken bones or other life-

threatening injuries. Dubbed the "Miracle [
Dosha even survived the subsequent media
that followed her ordeal, including an appear
with Matt Lauer on NBC's *Today* show.

Mutt Care and Maintenance

Mutts are hardy beasts. They are born hardy, having been crossbred, and they seem to get hardier with each blow that bad luck delivers. Still, mutts are only canine, which means that they are prone to, in the words of Shakespeare's Hamlet, every last one of the "thousand natural shocks/That flesh is heir to." They succumb to infection; they have accidents; they get bitten by ticks and mosquitoes. They require the same care as purebreds do. All dogs should see the vet once a year for a routine checkup, and at least once ideally twice) a year when they hit nine years of age, which marks the onset of old age in most dogs. A dog may need to see the vet at other times throughout the year if anything comes up.

Basic Maintenance

Puppies, like human babies, need lots of care and a host of shots throughout their first year. Most mutts are adopted as adults, after eight months of age, so your prime concern will often simply be maintenance.

Vaccinations

When a dog enters a shelter without proof of vaccination (current tags or medical records), he is automatically vaccinated. So if you adopt from a shelter, your dog will be up-to-date on his basic inoculations. If you adopt a stray, you'll have to err on the side of caution and have him vaccinated, especially if there are other animals at home. Once your pet is caught up, your vet will put him on a schedule. Although your dog needs a physical once a year (twice a year if he is more than nine years old), he only needs vaccination boosters every two to three years. Some vets will gladly charge you to vaccinate every year, but it's not necessary. Vaccines are designed to last longer than that. Discuss the schedule with your vet. The rabies vaccination is the only legally mandated inoculation. It's a good idea for dogs to wear a tag on their collars as proof of vaccination, so that in the event they become lost and wind up at a shelter, they're not needlessly revaccinated. In addition to rabies, every dog should receive a DHLPP (distemper, hepatitis, leptospirosis, parvovirus, parainfluenza virus) every two to three years. If your dog bites someone, or is accused of biting, and you can't prove he's been vaccinated, he will most likely be destroyed, so keeping the records is as important as getting the vaccination.

Some mutts should receive an additional leptospirosis vaccination. Leptospirosis is a bacterial disease spread by rodents, and the combination vaccine (DHLPP) does not cover all the different strains. If you live in a place with a serious rodent problem—usually deep in the country or deep in the city—ask your vet about this vaccine. Also, consider it a priority for some breed mixes. Terriers and Chihuahuas are notoriously passionate about rat flesh, dead or alive.

If you are planning to board your mutt at a kennel or leave him at dog day care, the host facility will require a vaccination against kennel cough (bordetella), which is administered through the nostril. Have this done at least two weeks before you plan to board your mutt.

Parasites

Fleas, ticks, worms, and other parasites are common to dogs who have had negligent medical care. Even well-cared-for dogs are susceptible if they're often outside, as country dogs are—especially to ticks and fleas. A particularly dangerous hazard is heartworm disease, a serious and potentially fatal condition caused by parasitic worms transmitted by a mosquito bite. Again, since they were living without shelter for a time, strays are very vulnerable. Heartworms (*Dirofilaria immitis*) live in the pulmonary arteries and hearts of infected animals. Untreated, the presence of these worms causes coughing, decreased energy, weight loss, and eventually heart and lung failure. Fortunately, heartworms are entirely preventable through regular testing and heartworm-preventive medication.

BUG OFF

Health nuts who don't wish to apply chemical pesticides directly to their mutts prefer to use a variety of natural preventives, including brewer's yeast sprinkled over dog food (it makes a dog's blood taste bad to bloodsucking pests) and herbal flea collars containing insect-repellent essential oils of lavender, pennyroyal, eucalyptus, and tea tree. As these methods are not always reliable, it's far better to use the natural insecticide diatomaceous earth, an odorless compound of finely milled fossilized shells of microorganisms (diatoms) that's nontoxic and safe for sprinkling directly into a dog's fur (or on his bedding, or anywhere else in the home where there's a potential pest problem). Here's how it works: The microscopically fine, sharp edges desiccate insects' exoskeleton upon contact, and bothersome pests—including fleas, bedbugs, flies, cockroaches, and ants—dehydrate and die within hours.

If you prefer to go a more traditional route, don't use a flea collar. They need to fit tightly in order to work, so they are uncomfortable for dogs. If they are too loose, they can be chewed off, and the poison they contain is highly toxic to dogs. Go instead with Frontline or Revolution, topical pesticides applied to a dog's shoulders, which work for fleas and ticks. If your dog has an adverse reaction—seizures have been documented in small animals treated with Frontline—discontinue use and consult your veterinarian without delay.

The first step is to have your dog's blood tested. If he tests positive, your vet will prescribe treatment; if the test comes back negative for heartworms, your vet will supply the preventive medication. Unlike most medications, this comes in a soft, palatable treat form that doesn't need to be disguised; dogs are happy to take it off your hands. Once a month on the same day, give your dog his heartworm medication "treat" according to the directions on the package, which comes with handy reminder stickers to put on your calendar.

Since heartworm is transmitted by mosquitos, and it's been diagnosed in dogs all over the United States and the world, heartworm preventive should be given during the months when it is warm enough for mosquitoes, which varies greatly across the United States. For example, if you live in or even travel with your dog regularly to a warm climate such as Florida, you should keep your dog on the preventive year-round. Your veterinarian will tell you what the heartworm season is in your location.

Lyme disease is spread by deer ticks in the Northeast and Midwest, and canines are just as susceptible as humans, if not more so, considering how much time they spend outdoors in the warm months. Take care to guard your dog by using some form of flea and tick control. If you suspect your mutt may have Lyme disease (the symptoms include lethargy and achy joints), have him seen by a vet, who will prescribe antibiotics.

Allergies

Following a discussion of horrors like rabies and heartworm, your dog's allergies may seem as non-threatening as the common cold. But allergies can be fatal, and mutts, despite their legendary hybrid vigor, are as at risk as any other dog. If your mutt has hives, or if he scratches himself a lot, chews on the tip of his tail, and bites and licks obsessively at his paw pads, he is showing classic signs of an allergic reaction. If you see any of these signs, rush your dog to the vet. If you're delayed getting to the vet and your dog is exploding in hives, administer over-the-counter diphenhydramine, a.k.a. Benadryl, at a dose of one milligram per pound of body weight. Each pill contains twenty-five milligrams, so one pill is enough for a twenty-five-pound mutt, and two are enough for a fifty-pounder. (Important: When giving a dog Benadryl, be sure that the pill you administer contains *only* diphenhydramine with no added ingredients such as ibuprofen or acetaminophen, which are both toxic and could result in death.) Sometimes, the treatment is as simple as a hypoallergenic diet such as Purina HA, made of hydrolyzed soy and available only by veterinary prescription. But often, getting to the root of a dog's allergies is a lot more complicated, involving microscopic examination of skin and hair samples and food trials to determine the exact culprit. To locate a veterinary allergy specialist, contact the American College of Veterinary Internal Medicine (ACVIM). Specialists are listed on their Web site, www.acvim.org.

To insure or not to insure?

Because you'll be seeing the vet several times a year, you might think that pet insurance is a good idea for you. I don't recommend it. Instead, I keep my mutts up-to-date on their care and keep a reserve fund of about $1,500 in case of an emergency. Obviously, no pet-insurance carrier is going to pay all your vet bills. (What would be in it for them?) And in fact, the deductible and between-the-lines restrictions of certain policies could wind up costing you more money, not to mention aggravation, than if you didn't have insurance in the first place. Besides, if your mutt is diagnosed with a catastrophic illness like cancer, the deductible will be eaten up by just one session of chemotherapy. And mutts are perceived as having pre-existing conditions that insurers believe they shouldn't have to pay for; carriers require a complete blood panel for all adult dogs. My advice is to skip pet insurance, make sure you have health insurance for yourself, and pay for mutt health care as you go along.

When to See a Vet

Be on the lookout for these warning signs, which may indicate that your dog is sick. If your mutt displays any of these symptoms, or any other out-of-the-ordinary condition that worries you, take him to a vet at once. A guide to twenty-four-hour emergency clinics can be found in the appendix, page 237. Here are some causes for alarm:

- ☐ Change in appetite, either more or less
- ☐ Change in energy level, either more or less
- ☐ Drinking more water
- ☐ Urinating more or not at all
- ☐ Diarrhea or constipation
- ☐ Vomiting
- ☐ Coughing
- ☐ Sneezing
- ☐ Discharge from the eyes, nose, or ears
- ☐ Ear scratching
- ☐ Scooting (i.e., dragging his butt on the ground)
- ☐ Excessive licking or biting at paws, tail, or other body parts

WARNING
you get what you pay for

Buy your pet's medications only from a veterinarian. You might be tempted to try a cheaper source, such as the Internet, but beware: E-tailers touting too-good-to-be-true offers are notorious for selling expired medications that won't do your dog any good—and could in fact cause harm.

Gour-Mutt Cuisine

All dog food is not created equal; you should buy only premium quality for your mutt. If you're not sure whether or not a dog food brand is premium quality, guide yourself by a simple rule: The cheaper a dog food is, the more likely it is to contain chemicals and other ingredients you wouldn't want to feed your mutt. Beaks, feathers, fur, tendons, and hooves all are technically protein, but they're not as nourishing as meat. "Protein" can also mean the rendered remains of euthanized shelter dogs, giving terrible new meaning to the expression, "you are what you eat." See the appendix (page 241) for some of my favorite premium dog food brands.

BONE APPÉTIT!

Where's my good-boy treat?

Wow! What's for dinner?

I just loved that frozen turkey dinner.

Kibbles! Yum!

Ho hum, I want what you are eating!

Tastes like chicken!

A **source of heated debate** in the canine-friendly community is kibble versus cans. Canned food contains fewer preservatives than kibble, and that's a big plus for mutts and strays who have had to subsist on a questionable diet of garbage picked off the street. They are already malnourished and have probably even

There are high-quality brands of kibble out there; check the label to be sure they're preserved with tocopherol (vitamin E) instead of ethoxyquin (a known carcinogen).

Strays are already malnourished and have probably even swallowed trace amounts of motor oil, gasoline, and other toxic substances found on the street or in trash dumps.

swallowed trace amounts of motor oil, gasoline, and other toxic substances found on the street or in trash dumps. If you take care to feed your mutt or stray premium-quality food with minimal preservatives, the transformation you will notice in his liveliness will be eye-opening. Of course, kibble is certainly more convenient than cans.

Of late, some companies have begun manufacturing condiments to pour over dog kibble to make it more palatable. Rather than adding still more preservatives to your mutt's diet, why not pour olive oil or flaxseed oil over the kibble instead? You probably already have these oils in your cupboard, they're great for your dog's skin and coat, and they enhance the flavor of anything—yes, even dry kibble.

Gringo, rescued as a stray by photographer Mary Ellen Mark, is served birthday table scraps.

Some mutts have iron stomachs; others struggle with delicate digestive systems that are easily upset by the slightest dietary variation. When making alterations to your dog's diet, don't make a radical food change too abruptly, or you could wind up smelling canine flatulence or cleaning up canine diarrhea. If your mutt is already on, say, a lower grade of lamb-based food that agrees with him, start by switching over slowly to a high-quality food (without ethoxyquin) in which the main ingredi-

ent is also lamb. Any dietary changes should be made gradually, by adding more and more of the new food to your mutt's old food over the course of seven to ten days (start with one-third new to two-thirds old; then two-thirds new to one-third old; then all new food). And it's always a good idea to supplement prepackaged dog food, whether it comes from a bag or a can, with regular helpings of fresh, cooked meat and raw or cooked vegetables as often as you can.

What No Dog Should Eat

If you suspect your dog may have ingested one or more of the following, run, don't walk, to the animal hospital's emergency room:

- Over-the-counter human medications (one Aleve, Advil, or Tylenol can kill a dog from intestinal bleeding)
- Antifreeze
- Cocoa mulch and other fertilizers
- Prescription medication for humans
- Desitin ointment
- AlternaGEL antacid
- Alcohol
- Illegal recreational drugs
- Chocolate or any product containing it, especially bittersweet chocolate used for baking, which contains high levels of theobromine (it's highly toxic to dogs)
- Coffee, tea, or anything containing caffeine
- Houseplants, especially any species of lily
- Grapes, raisins, or any cereal, pastry, or other food containing raisins (they cause kidney failure)
- Gum (the main ingredient of sugarless chewing gum, xylitol, is poisonous to dogs)

ATTENTION ANIMAL ACTIVISTS

The organization People for the Ethical Treatment of Animals (PETA) was established in 1980 to defend animals against cruelty and has grown to become the largest organization of its kind, with more than 850,000 members worldwide. If you are concerned about animal safety, log on to the PETA site (www.peta.org) or its companion site (www.caringconsumer.com). You will see lists of companies that do and do not test on animals, and you might be shocked at what you find—for instance, the pet food giant Iams has been found to test on animals. Many consumers now boycott the brand.

Besides leaving them vulnerable to parasites and other pests, a life on the street teaches strays to be perpetually on the lookout for a snack. More precisely, it imprints on them a hunger as indelible as a tattoo. All dogs are opportunists when it comes to snatching up food scraps, but with mutts, the drive is much stronger than with purebreds who never had to fend for themselves. Even when they are handsomely fed at home, mutts will view any outing as a chance to expand their dining options. While amusing at first, the mutt's never-ending quest for extra victuals poses certain serious health hazards—obesity and poisoning not least among them—that mutt people need to be aware of.

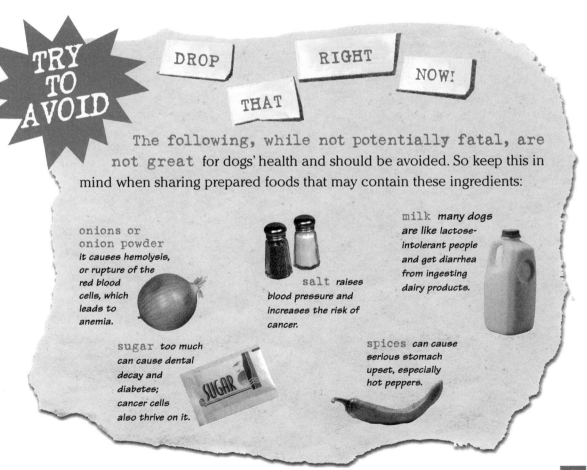

TRY TO AVOID

DROP RIGHT NOW!

THAT

The following, while not potentially fatal, are not great for dogs' health and should be avoided. So keep this in mind when sharing prepared foods that may contain these ingredients:

onions or onion powder *it causes hemolysis, or rupture of the red blood cells, which leads to anemia.*

salt *raises blood pressure and increases the risk of cancer.*

milk *many dogs are like lactose-intolerant people and get diarrhea from ingesting dairy products.*

sugar *too much can cause dental decay and diabetes; cancer cells also thrive on it.*

spices *can cause serious stomach upset, especially hot peppers.*

What Bailey Ate

Bailey lived with my friend Susan Ainsworth in Miami and, later, New York. From the time she found him as a puppy on a Puerto Rico street until he died at age eleven and a half, he was (like all mutts) a true omnivore. "When Bailey was a tiny pup, he had two diets: an 'official' one of organic dry dog food, mixed with some people things, and the shadow diet of things he got into when no one was looking," Susan explains. Here's a partial inventory of what Bailey ate:

Potrait of Bailey by Martha Szabo

- Roach traps (two boxes at one sitting, prompting a frantic call to poison control)

- Shoes, the strappier and pricier the better (he never went for a loafer, but really loved a good Manolo)

- Lipstick and other makeup (at the time, Susan was enamored of Aveda lip colors, which have a slightly spicy taste and fragrance)

- Paper products, including napkins, towels, toilet paper, tampons (did they help with teething?)

- Cassette tapes (dozens of them)

- Anything that had ever been in the garbage (chicken carcasses, coffee grounds and filters, pizza crusts, a pound of frozen raw hamburger meat)

- Plastic baggies

- Seaweed and dead fish on the beach (pretty)

- Bar soap (he would chew on it and literally foam at the mouth)

MARISA
MARCHETTO

A food tip

If you find yourself out of dog food and the pet supply store is closed, don't break down and buy low-grade supermarket brands. Boil some chicken in plain water, debone it thoroughly, combine it with plain rice, and pour some of the boiled broth over it all (skim the fat off first). Let cool and serve at room temperature. Or purchase a few jars of baby food—chicken or beef flavor—and combine with fresh white rice from your local Chinese takeout. One-stop-shopping tip: Pet supply stores aren't the only place to buy pet food; Whole

Foods and small, local health food stores also carry premium brands of dog food.

There's an important difference between well fed and overfed: You should be able to see the outline of your mutt's rib cage, and she should have a defined waistline (just like a human who's in good shape). Besides putting your mutt at risk for heart disease and diabetes, packing on pounds means carrying around extra weight, which causes undue strain on the joints. Many large mutts who are overweight suffer torn cruciate ligaments, which require expensive surgery and a several-months-long recovery period involving severely restricted movement.

HOME COOKING ON THE RUN

Here's a convenient shortcut for those who'd like to cook for their dogs but don't have much time: Dr. Harvey's Canine Health is a premix formula; combine it with oil and plain, boiled meat, and serve.

Cleanliness Is Next to Dogliness

Beauty is more than skin deep to be sure—but even the most photogenic mutt needs your help to come clean.

Because purebred dogs such as poodles and Malteses are frequent flyers at the professional groomer's, emerging with snow-white coats accented with ribbons and bows, many people think dog grooming is a frivolous subject. But it's not just about beauty; it's an essential part of caring for your mutt that directly affects his health. Just like people, dogs have beneficial oils in their skin that protect them from infection, but too much oil buildup on hair dulls its sheen. Plus, if they've been playing outdoors, mutts are also wearing grass stains, mud, sand, sea salt, and even automotive grease. Besides coming off on your furniture, these substances can cause skin problems if not cleansed away, or harm to the dog if he licks them off. Don't be overzealous in bathing your dog; too-frequent cleansing can overdry his skin, leaving it open to infection. Bathe your dog only when necessary—when you notice that he smells bad or has a dirty coat. Be sure the shampoo you use on your mutt is formulated for pets; don't use ordinary human shampoo, as it will have a different pH balance. If your mutt absolutely hates being bathed, do him and yourself a favor by sending him to a reputable professional groomer.

WASH ME!

GEE, MY COAT SMELLS TERRIFIC.

dog's ears prior to wetting him down, then remove the cotton after the final rinse). And never poke cotton swabs down into a mutt's ear canal; ask your vet for a demonstration of how to safely clean canine ears.

Otherwise, wear an old T-shirt and shorts and do it yourself in the bathtub or backyard—it's a fun bonding experience. While you're lathering up, scan your mutt's body carefully for any skin abnormalities or lumps. If you encounter anything suspicious, have it checked by a vet without delay. To avoid the canine equivalent of swimmer's ear, always end baths with a gentle ear cleaning (for extra safety, place protective cotton in your

Lather, rinse, repeat

Advances in human hair care have bubbled over to dog beauty products. Many incorporate luxury ingredients like shea butter and organic essential oils. A far cry from the harsh, detergenty dog shampoos of yore! Here are some of my favorite brands:

Mellow Mutts. This line contains calming organic essential oils.

SheaPet. Their shampoos contain moisturizing shea butter for mutts prone to dry coats.

Fauna. A collection of grooming products made from naturally antiseptic ingredients such as lavender, grapefruit, and tea tree oil. It's for canine coats *and* human hair.

Aesop Animal. This shampoo contains fragrant mint oil and the apothecary-style glass bottle is chic, if extremely breakable.

The author and her red-coated mutt, Sheba, after Julia had her hair colored to match the dog's.

ALL IN THE FAMILY

For some, grooming is a family affair. I have always admired my border collie mix Sheba's rich auburn coat. One day it struck me that I could more than admire it—I could have that look myself. So I brought Sheba to the Julien Farel Salon and had my hair dyed to match.

Paw-di-cure

Mutts' nails should be trimmed regularly to keep paws in good shape. Some dogs, especially dogs with short legs—think corgi and dachshund mixes—*hate* having this done. For these dogs, it's best to leave this chore to the vet or professional groomer. If your dog will let you trim his nails, buy a clipper (it will look like a pair of pliers) and take off just the tips of the nails every couple of months. You might want to buy some styptic powder along with the clippers—if you clip too aggressively and hit the quick (the vein that runs down the middle of the nail), the nail will bleed profusely.

nail
clipper

Brush up!

Dogs benefit from regular tooth brushing as well. Mutts are particularly prone to dental problems as many have had unorthodox diets. Some have eaten too much sugary people food and have suffered from calculus buildup that causes tooth decay. Others have eaten dangerous nonfood products, which can give them gum problems and wear down dental enamel. And most haven't had regular checkups. Brush your dog's teeth with a finger toothbrush and canine toothpaste, which comes in a variety of delicious flavors, including chicken. Try to brush your dog's teeth a few times a week, or at the very least once weekly, to keep tartar at bay. If your dog ever has to be put under anesthesia for any reason, ask the vet if you can have his teeth cleaned and polished at the same time.

tooth
tool

Home Away from Home

While you're away at work, you'll need to make sure your mutt gets walked so he can relieve himself and get some exercise. This is important for his mental and physical health. You can hire a dog walker, but take care not to entrust your dog to anyone who makes a practice of handling more than two dogs at one time. So-called pack walks endanger the dogs being walked.

An increasingly popular way to keep mutts busy and safe while you're at the office or out of town is to drop them off at one of the country's swank doggie day care facilities, such as Chicago's Bow Wow Lounge, The Common Dog in Boston, and Portland's Urban Fauna. The accommodations at these places include large outdoor runs, where dogs exercise and socialize with each other; Astroturf-carpeted indoor runs for inclement weather; and sofas for canine couch potatoes. Guardians who worry that their mutt might become injured or ill can rest easy knowing that some day care facilities have on-call vets (and New York's Brooklyn Dog House is part owned by a vet). WoofSpa and Resort, located in Manhattan's fashionable meatpacking district, is a veritable Club Med for canines, with sleek architecture that could easily lead one to mistake it for a chic boutique hotel. For an extra charge, WoofSpa will escort your best friend to Bonnie's K9 Corp., New York's only heated pool just for dogs, for swim sessions and hydromassage.

Spa-a-ah treatment

THE DOG SONG

Mutt Mavens now have an anthem thanks to Nellie McKay. The singer-songwriter was inspired by her beloved mutt Joey to write "The Dog Song," whose lyrics go, in part: "If you need a companion / Well just go right to the pound / And find yourself a hound / And make that doggie proud." Joey, found as a stray when McKay was 10 years old, was musically quite opinionated. "He never liked my music," McKay says of the black Lab-Doberman-chow mix. "When I sang, he mainly just gave me a dirty look and left the room! He had very distinct tastes."

Downward-facing dog

Imagine how your poor mutt feels: She's separated from you all day while you're at work and is waiting anxiously for your return. Then you finally arrive home, and—you rush off to the gym. Parted again! If that's your routine, it's time to change it by practicing the postures and breathing exercises of yoga with a beloved mutt by your side. Dogs don't need to learn yoga; they do it instinctively. Ever notice how a dog takes time to stretch after a nap? He's doing yoga. So why not make your pet your guru? To help people follow a home yoga regimen, I've listed a couple of books on the subject (see appendix, page 243).

Music to soothe the savage beast

California harpist Susan Raimond noticed, while playing one day at the harp shop where she works, that all the dogs on the premises crowded around her and promptly, blissfully conked out, including Jackson, her own beloved rottweiler-Doberman mix. Soon after that, Raimond recorded *Wait for the Sunset,* one of five soothing CDs of harp music she's compiled to calm anxious animals at shelters, hospitals, and zoos. From dogs and cats to birds and giraffes, all have succumbed to slumber minutes after the music starts playing.

You are getting very slee-e-epy . . .

Alternative Medicine

Like all mutts,
Ruby is a yoga natural.

Many people of late have been combining traditional and alternative medicine for a hybrid approach to their own health. And many dog people seem to believe that the hybrid approach to health care is also the way to go with a hybrid dog; vets around the country are even starting to combine traditional veterinary medicine with other "modalities" in their practices. Homeopathy, acupuncture, Chinese herbal medicine, massage therapy, gem therapy, Reiki, Acutonics—any alternative therapy that applies to adventurous humans

> ### PET-IQUETTE
> Never call dogs "it." Please refer to mutts and all animals as "him" or "her."

seems to apply equally well to mutts. These gentle procedures are especially helpful to mutts who have suffered abuse or abandonment. Some believe that applying these therapies to shelter dogs can calm them, enabling them to transcend the stress of the shelter environment and get adopted more quickly. Vicki Draper, who practices craniosacral therapy and Jin Shin acupressure in Portland, Oregon, recalls that the first dog she worked on was a pit bull mix at a local shelter who had been in residence for three months with no takers. A few days after her session with Draper, the dog was adopted.

GOT MY EYE ON YOU

Actress Selma Blair is part of a proud young Hollywood elite that believes in rescuing mutts and showering them with attention (her peers include Christian Bale, Drew Barrymore, Jake Gyllenhaal, Orlando Bloom, Rachael Leigh Cook, Kate Bosworth, Matt LeBlanc, and Lake Bell). Blair adopted her one-eyed mutt, Wink, from the Lange Foundation, where, she says, "They have the most amazing misfit dogs in the world . . . mostly older dogs whose owners died, dogs where you could throw a book at them and they'd read it. They're completely the cutest and sweetest dogs." Blair hated the idea of leaving Wink behind while she was filming in Prague for three long months—so she boarded the mutt at Los Angeles's Loved Dog. A new breed of deluxe kennel offering "cage-free sleepovers," where guests have their own rooms and are free to roam, Loved Dog is happy to e-mail photographs to a dog's family during his or her stay. Blair also called Loved Dog every day from Prague to check up on Wink, so she wouldn't forget her voice.

NOTE BOOK

NOTE BOOK

SLEEPOVER RX

If you're prepared to go to extreme measures with an ailing mutt, the Center for Specialized Veterinary Care in Westbury, New York, offers the country's first facility where people can stay overnight while their pet undergoes treatment. "Evidence shows that animals heal faster with their families," says the center's founder, Dr. Diane Levitan. So she turned one wing of her hospital into the Compassionate Care Center. Cozy rooms are equipped with a platform bed for dogs and a recliner for humans, plus a TV, sink, desk, and Internet connection. Other services offered include acupuncture, hydrotherapy, car service to pick up clients from all five boroughs of New York, and bereavement counseling.

Saying Good-Bye

Mutts may cheat death many times, but death always wins in the end. If your mutt is suffering great physical pain, don't prolong his life in a selfish, sentimental attempt to hold on to him. Many people understandably have an aversion to the concept of euthanasia, especially since it is used to destroy perfectly healthy young mutts in overcrowded animal shelters. But in the case of a terminally ill dog, euthanasia can be a blessing.

The ides of august

In August of 2004, I decided to put my mutt, Hound, to sleep. One day, the spry little fellow was fourteen years going on fourteen months, leaping vertically at the first scent of food and generally behaving as if he were getting younger every day. The next, he was walking helplessly in circles and falling sideways, his head at an extreme tilt, his eyes rolling frighteningly fast in his head. The vet diagnosed Hound's problem: Canine geriatric vestibular syndrome, which attacks the organ of balance, sending it off-kilter. Basically, it was making my poor Hound feel like he was on a high-speed merry-go-round from hell. The syndrome has no cause and no cure, and frequently strikes in the month of August (no one knows why, but for me this factoid gave sad new meaning to the term "dog days of August"). I had the option of waiting, with a fifty-fifty chance that the condition might clear up with time. If it didn't, he'd be permanently, outrageously uncomfortable. But Hound was old, so there was less of a chance he would bounce back. All the while, Hound looked desperately miserable. I waited a couple of days, but he could barely manage to eat the small morsels of freshly cooked chicken and duck I offered him. That's how I knew he was really suffering; he just wasn't himself. It is difficult to know when it's time to put a dog to sleep; vets often say, "You will know," but it's easy to keep clinging to the hope that things will turn around and your dog will be his old self again. In this case, somehow I sensed Hound would not. The mutt who just days before was defying gravity to jump for scraps of roast chicken was physically unable to accept my relentless offers of chicken, bacon, roast beef, and baby food. His appetite was officially gone, and, I suspected, his appetite for life had gone with it. We took him to the vet. When the injection was administered, he passed so peacefully, closing his rolling eyes with such evident

relief, that I knew I'd made the right decision. After days and days of terrible dizziness, he seemed genuinely grateful to get some rest at last.

AARP? arf!

Elderly pets abound at shelters, and they're a terrific match for retired people or those who just don't feel like meeting the physical demands of a high-energy canine athlete. Senior dogs bond strongly with adopters because they seem to know this is a last chance at love. Senior dogs also tend to be trained in the basics; they're calmer; and they don't chew or scratch at every object that crosses their path. They don't run; they walk. For those who prefer a leisurely stroll through the park over a high-speed run, a senior mutt's low-key pace is ideal. Besides, it's well documented that dogs help people live longer, healthier lives, so adopting a mutt could be just the thing to get a senior person motivated to stay in shape.

Mutts are a terrific match for retired people

Old Dogs, New Tricks

While mutts are often healthier than purebreds, they do not have a natural leg up over purebreds in the obedience department. Mixed breeds require the same amount of basic training as any other dog to make them well-behaved canine citizens. And many mutts or formerly homeless purebreds may have picked up bad habits that need to be unlearned. But one of the many advantages of mutts is their eminent trainability and retrainability. Mutts are remarkably adaptable; in exchange for being part of your life, they are happy to learn from you and improve themselves.

BERT

Whether **you adopt from a shelter** or rescue a stray, you will find out very quickly just how much training your mutt has had and how many bad behaviors will need to be eliminated or redirected (that's dog-training-speak for "unlearned").

Depending on age and history, a mutt can be quite well behaved or be an unruly bundle of raw energy with no training at all. The type of animal shelter you adopt from plays a part, too; if a mutt has been in residence at a no-kill shelter where a behaviorist donates time to train the dogs, he will already have been exposed to some of the basics, such as how to sit. At a kill shelter, there is little to no opportunity to work with dogs on training, so the range of behavior is much more mixed.

But one thing is certain: No matter where they come from or what their level of training, most mutts are intelligent and eager to please, making them wonderful students of obedience. Animal trainers and behaviorists actually prefer working with mutts because of their willingness to do any task you give them, rather than one specialized task that the average purebred is genetically programmed to perform, like hunting. In a word, mutts are versatile. They adapt brilliantly to the task at hand, whether it's assisting a person with disabilities or acting on stage.

> "I like a bit of a mongrel myself, whether it's a man or a dog; they're the best for every day."
>
> —George Bernard Shaw

Mutts are quick to learn, and happy to help teach. Sinbad the Afghan mix (below) appears in fundraising campaigns for the California State Firefighters Association Education Fund. He also inspires his human, illustrator Betsy Baytos, to draw educational comics for kids. In one comic, Sinbad teaches campfire safety alongside a pop-culture icon: Smokey Bear.

If you adopted your mutt from a big city animal shelter, you may find she has command of a tongue other than the one she kisses you with. Some mutts prick up their ears when they catch snippets of conversations in other languages, such as Spanish. If you find that your mutt is fluent in a language you don't speak, why not get a phrase book and try speaking to your dog in her mother tongue?

Arroz con pollo, por favor.

Mutts excel in the entertainment field, especially on stage, where there are no retakes. They also excel at search and rescue, drug detection, therapy work, and assisting the physically challenged as service dogs. But most of all, mutts make excellent family pets, because their focus is not on hunting or herding or guarding—it's on pleasing their families. Mixed-breed dogs are happy to adjust their routines to fit into a family's routine. Versatility is the mutt's greatest asset, and that versatility is what makes mixed-breed dogs highly trainable.

Training a mutt is much more than a chore; it's a fine way to bond with your dog and enhance your quality time together. The better behaved a mutt is, the more easily you can take him with you when you leave the house, and the more places you can see together on your mutt journey.

¿Que pasa?

¡Vamos!

Tequiero, perrito.

RANDOM HOUSE WEBSTER'S

POCKET

Spanish

DICTIONARY

Englis

Crate Expectations

One of the beauties of mutts is that many come housebroken. If your mutt lived with a family, chances are she will only need a brief refresher, if any help at all, with housebreaking. And if she was a stray, her time on the street will inspire her to respect the great indoors.

If you find your mutt does need help, buy a training crate. It's the best housebreaking tool. The principle of the crate is this: Because dogs don't go to the bathroom where they sleep, and they view the crate as their own little den, they won't soil it. The crate helps train a dog to "go" outside by teaching her to hold it until you can get her outside to the appropriate elimination area. Do not crate a mutt under eight months, however; their muscles aren't developed enough to hold it. Use Wee-Wee Pads (see appendix, page 245) —a more effective and sanitary alternative to newspaper—until your pup is old enough to graduate to the crate.

Puppies under five months should be confined in one area of a room, using a baby barrier. Line the area (basically, diaper the floor) with Wee-Wee Pads. Wee-Wee Pads are more absorbent than newspaper, and dogs prefer to urinate on absorbent, nonporous surfaces because their urine won't splash back on them. (This is also why puppies prefer to pee on carpets rather than on hard floors, so to protect your carpeting, keep very young pups away from it.) Once your puppy reaches eight months, abandon the Wee-Wee Pads; you are ready for housebreaking and crate training.

Crates are made of metal wire (plastic kennels with wire-mesh panels are designed for transporting dogs and should not be confused with training crates), so many people mistakenly view the training crate as a prison. It isn't, and it should not be turned into one. The key to successful crate use is selecting the correct one and using it properly. The crate must be large enough for your dog to turn around in comfortably, stand up without banging his head, and lie down. It should be kept clean; most crate models come with a tray that slides out for ease of cleaning. A crate should also be something you don't mind looking at. Many models come powder-coated in black, green, or other colors, so they look less out of place in your home. These tend to be more expensive than the no-frills metal variety. So some people drape attractive fabric across the top of their plain-Jane crate. Whatever you do, don't keep your dog's crate away from the family action or in the basement; this will defeat the purpose of the crate and result in a lonely, stressed-out dog. If situated "out of sight, out of mind," the crate *does* become a prison.

A den of one's own

Introduce your dog to his crate as a positive thing with a treat. This will become his room in your home, and he will come to like it. Crate training works like this: The dog spends two to three hours at a time in the crate until he understands that home is not a place to go to the bathroom, nor a place to chew up and destroy. After each sojourn in the

We are a litter of rottie-shepherds.

Look at our different markings.

crate, take the dog outside and encourage him to relieve himself. When he does, praise him, say "good dog," and give him a treat the first few times. He will associate eliminating outside with a reward. When you return inside, by all means play with the dog and spend time with him outside of the crate. When you have finished playing with the dog, return him to the crate for an hour or two. Then take him outside again.

The dog should sleep in the crate, too. The goal is to be able to leave the crate door open so that Fido can retreat to it when he pleases, not when you tell him to.

> Never jail a dog in his crate as punishment, and never use the crate for long-term confinement.

Never jail a dog in his crate as punishment, and never use the crate for long-term confinement. Making a dog do more than four hours of crate time at a stretch (except during the night) is simply wrong, comparable to forcing a large, tall person to sit in the middle economy seat of an airplane all day. The crate is a temporary training tool, not a place to stash your dog when you just don't feel like dealing with him. Also, remember that the inside of the crate should be just comfortable enough. Don't make your dog's crate too cozy, with food and water bowls and chew toys and pillows; all those accessories simply defeat the purpose of training, which is to

Some of us are mostly tan, others black.

But we all have black-tipped tails!

teach him to respect his home. If you give him all the soft comforts of home in the crate, he won't have any incentive to learn the difference between out here and in there. Be patient; in time, the crate will be a thing of the past for both of you, and you'll be sharing the fine furniture with safety and ease.

Time spent on crate training will vary from mutt to mutt. With a puppy, use the crate for two to four weeks, until he's old enough to hold it long enough to go outside. With an adult mutt, use the crate for one to three weeks at the most.

Why a designer crate?

Even though a crate-trained **mutt** is much less likely to wind up at an animal shelter "because he wrecked the house," there are many people who remain convinced that it's wrong to keep a dog in a cage even for a minute. Being abandoned is obviously the more cruel fate, and it's completely avoidable when

crates are used regularly and humanely. The trouble is that most crate manufacturers don't take design into account, so crates wind up looking the way the anti-crate camp perceives them: like mini-prisons. It took several years, but finally a talented architect tackled the dog crate problem, transforming it from an eyesore into an attractive, sculptural object that actually enhances a room. The brainchild of Canadian architect Katrina Herrndorf, the Bowhaus is a sleek metal oval with decoratively perforated sides. It looks chic and doubles as a small table in the hippest interiors. With this crate option, dogs won't miss out on the action while doing necessary crate time, and you won't miss out on stylish decor while you train.

The Bowhaus proves that a crate can be stylish enough to be prominently displayed wherever the family action is.

MUTTROPOLIS

San Francisco—fittingly, the city named for Saint Francis, the patron saint of animals—is the closest place on Earth to a promised land for mutts. One in ten households donates to the local SPCA, bringing public and private spending on animal welfare to about $10 a person each year (versus $1.70, the national per-person average for major cities). This enables the city to euthanize only 25 percent of its impounded animals, the lowest figure of any major U.S. city. What's more, mutts awaiting their homes at Maddie's Pet Adoption Center, the San Francisco SPCA's sparkling shelter designed by ARQ Architects, do their waiting in cozy rooms outfitted with sofas, TVs, and aquariums in lieu of impersonal metal cages. When taken out to exercise and socialize with others of their kind, San Francisco mutts don't play in mere dog runs; they romp in off-leash areas (OLAs for short). There's more: Here, the law says mutts are not property, they're companions, and the people they live with are not dog owners, but guardians. That ordinance was passed into law in 2003 by the San Francisco Board of Supervisors, which voted to change city codes to include the word guardians wherever "pet owners" are mentioned. "We're really trying to get to the heart of trying to treat animals more humanely and promote guardianship," said Matt Gonzalez, the board's president and chief sponsor of the ordinance. Incidentally, San Francisco wasn't the first city to legislate the evolution of pet owners to guardians. Boulder, Colorado, was the first U.S. city to make pet owners guardians, followed by Berkeley and West Hollywood and the state of Rhode Island. Colorado and California are among fourteen states legally recognizing dogs and cats as beneficiaries and allowing people to leave money and property to pets in their wills.

From Muttropolis with Love

PARCEL POST

Basic Commands

After housebreaking, it's time to move on to basic training. All dogs should be able to obey the four essential commands:

heel

sit

stay

come

The most important is heel,

which ensures that your dog stays beside you on a leash, at a pace that's comfortable for you, whether you're walking or running. Whether you live in an urban, suburban, or rural setting, you should walk your mutt on a leash. It is not a good idea to let your dog walk without a leash, especially if he was previously a stray; if spooked, he could take off in an instant. Part of attaching yourself to any dog is tethering him to you with a leash. But that principle is especially important with mutts, many of whom are used to wandering. Let your mutt off the leash if you're certain he has no chance of escape—in a yard or a dog run with a high fence.

How you attach your leash to your dog is up to you. The most common method is with a collar made of nylon or leather. Some dogs, however, have endured the trauma of having metal collars become embedded in the skin on their neck through neglect, requiring surgical removal. If that is the case with your mutt, it is kinder to use a harness, which won't rub against his neck, reminding him of that old injury.

But a harness—which is a fancy leash that goes over the dog's shoulders—gives you much less control over a dog than a collar. It actually increases the force of a dog's pull, and if the dog pulls hard, that can be hazardous to both of you. Many dogs can pull several times their own weight, prompting wisecracking passersby to ask, "Who's walking whom?" But it's no joke: A dog who pulls too hard is a serious problem. Upon sighting a pigeon or squirrel, large dogs can easily lift a person right off his feet, especially in inclement weather. And if the walker loses his grip on the leash, the dog could run into traffic or get lost in the woods or, if he's dog-aggressive, get into a fight with another dog that could result in injury on both sides. One traditional cure for pulling was metal "choke" or "pinch" collars, which apply pressure to a dog's throat and can cause tracheal damage if used incorrectly.

Dog lovers who shun metal collars opt instead for a head halter such as the Gentle Leader, which attaches to a dog's snout and works very well at curtailing a dog's pulling capability. It also comes with an excellent manual that's a fine primer on beginning dog training. But some people don't like the fact that head halters resemble muzzles, giving even poodles an intimidating appearance. What's more, while head halters are not painful, some dogs find them annoying and spend half their walk time pitifully trying to claw or rub the things off. If your dog can tolerate the Gentle Leader, it's a fine training tool.

If your dog is bothered by it, an excellent solution is the Softouch SENSE-ation harness, which has become quite popular with professional dog trainers. It's a nylon device that attaches low around a dog's chest, almost like a bra, yet it hinders pulling equally well by applying pressure to the dog's shoulders. The leash clips to a ring on the harness's chest strap. The harness works well on all sizes of dogs; unlike the head halter, dogs don't mind the way it feels, and handlers can easily maintain control of the strongest dogs while walking them. In every respect, the SENSE-ation harness is ideal for mutts, especially large ones who may have experienced trauma with collars.

The other basic commands--sit, stay, and come—are more than just tricks for a dog to perform, they could save your dog's life if he should ever become separated from you while still in your sight. Let's say your dog's collar snaps off in the middle of a busy city intersection, or the hatch of your car inexplicably flies open, and your intrepid mutt jumps out and trots off into the middle of a city street (both horrors have happened to me). In these cases, you and your mutt are connected by one thing and one thing only: your voice. So if you say "sit" or "stay" or "come" and mean it, and you've trained your dog to comply with these commands, you've saved his life.

Two other useful ones are "leave it" and "drop it." These come in especially handy if, say, a dog picks up something nasty off the street and proceeds to devour it.

How to Train Your Mutt

Training has evolved to the point where now everyone agrees that positive reinforcement is the best way to train. Punitive methods, besides being cruel and outdated, simply don't work well on any dog, especially mutts. Think back to Psychology 101 pillars Pavlov and Skinner: They got better results from their subjects by using rewards than they did with punishment. We've since learned that everyone, two-legged and four-legged, responds better to this kind of gentle, gradual conditioning.

For example, let's say a dog jumps up on people a lot. Rather than saying "no" or "down" every time the dog jumps, ignore the dog when he jumps. As soon as he is not jumping, lavish praise on him and offer a treat. It's important to give your praise and treat just as he is displaying the desired behavior. If you wait too long afterward, your desire will not be communicated. You need to continue to praise the good behavior for several weeks, until your mutt understands that good behavior is the fastest way to a delicious treat. Eventually, when your mutt really gets it, you can drop the treat. The praise will be incentive

Ring any bells? Pavlov and his research subject.

CLASS SCHEDULE

NAME Skipper   **SCHOOL** Collie Cross College

ADDRESS

PERIOD	MONDAY		TUESDAY		WEDNESDAY		THURSDAY		FRIDAY
	SUBJECT	ROOM	SUBJECT	ROOM	SUBJECT	ROOM	SUBJECT	ROOM	SUBJECT
1	psychology 101								
2	animal behavior								
3	snack break								
4	advanced positive reinforcement								
5	recess								
6									

enough. Be consistent: If you slack off and pat and praise the dog sometimes when he jumps up, he'll be confused.

Since mutts are such food junkies—er, connoisseurs—not just any food will do; the motivation has to be something *really* tasty, such as freshly baked chicken breast, turkey, or hot dogs. Don't bother with the hard treats sold in boxes at supermarkets. Those are high in carbohydrates, and your mutt is not a carbivore,

he's a carnivore. The way to motivate him is with meat—soft, chewy, delicious-smelling meat. So consider preparing your own meaty snacks or, if that's not possible, seek out tried-and-true motivators such as chewy, fragrant Solid Gold Tiny Tots Jerky Dog Treats; in my house, the mere sight of these has been known to get dogs to sit without even being told (see appendix, page 245 for a list of highly palatable training treats).

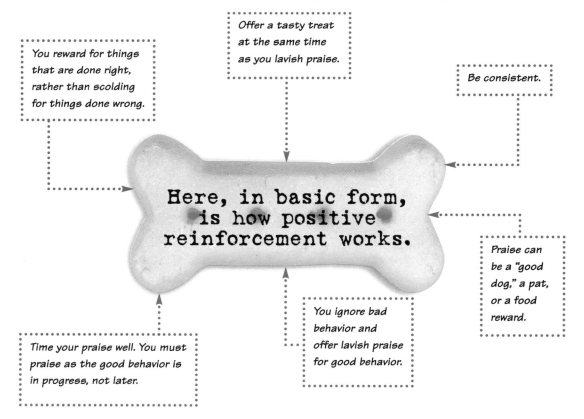

You reward for things that are done right, rather than scolding for things done wrong.

Offer a tasty treat at the same time as you lavish praise.

Be consistent.

Here, in basic form, is how positive reinforcement works.

Praise can be a "good dog," a pat, or a food reward.

Time your praise well. You must praise as the good behavior is in progress, not later.

You ignore bad behavior and offer lavish praise for good behavior.

"I believe that training dogs actually makes them smarter,"

says the eminent naturalist Hope Ryden. She used positive reinforcement to teach her mutt, Chloe, to perform a repertoire of parlor tricks, including "Play the piano."

Training and your dog's past

Your mutt has a past. He may come with no emotional baggage at all or he may have "issues." Sometimes the issues stay dormant, and other times they make themselves known—usually at the least opportune moments. For instance, say that as you are walking down the street, a rollerblader whizzes by and your mutt lunges for him. Behavior like this is obviously not acceptable and must be redirected.

THERE ARE SOME THINGS YOU CAN DO.

First, try basic training methods. Be patient and diligent and see if you can redirect the unwanted behaviors.

Second, try avoidance. For instance, if you dog is terrified of traffic noises and you live in a big city, try walking him not at rush hour, but at other times.

Third, look for creative solutions. If your dog is randomly aggressive on the leash, you might be surprised that she's sociable and polite in the dog run when she's off-leash. (Of course, the first several times you go to the dog run, you should be prepared for the worst. Go at a low-traffic time of day and be very watchful.)

Fourth, seek professional help. If your mutt turns out to have serious aggression or extreme timidity or other strong and strange personality quirks, you really should consult a trainer. (See appendix, page 245, for how to find a reputable trainer.)

If your mutt is part coyote, like Poe, he is likely to take "Don't Fence Me In" as his motto.

It's important to train him to comply with "sit," "stay," and "come" so you have a chance of seeing him again in the event that he heeds the call of the wild and takes off.

Cave canem

Muzzling is not a good training tool. It's a quick fix that doesn't actually fix anything. It exacerbates the problem: A dog with an aggression problem will feel more insecure and behave even more aggressively in a muzzle. If you absolutely have to use a muzzle, use one with a wire cage that prevents the dog's teeth from making contact with a person or another dog, yet still permits the dog to breathe and open his mouth. Nylon muzzles that only permit a hole for the nostrils should never be used outside of a vet's office.

Metal collars are another punitive quick-fix method. There are several types of metal collars, which are used as training devices. "Pinch" or "prong" collars have metal spikes that dig into a dog's neck when he pulls too hard; this kind of collar should never be used on a puppy, and absolutely must be removed when the dog is relaxing at home, as it's extremely uncomfortable and prevents your dog from lying down. The choke collar, on the other hand—a metal chain that fits around a dog's neck—is the subject of much controversy.

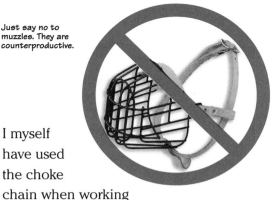

Just say no to muzzles. They are counterproductive.

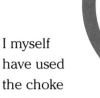

I myself have used the choke chain when working with very strong, potentially aggressive dogs. It's not my first choice, but it can work at the beginning of training (never for the life of the dog). There are correct and incorrect ways to use it; it's only cruel when misused. Always position the chain high on the dog's neck so that when you make the correction by tugging or pulling quickly on the chain, you're not harming the dog's windpipe and causing him tracheal damage, which in severe cases results in permanent breathing and swallowing difficulty. Never use a choke collar on a puppy, and always remove this type of collar when your dog is crated, as dogs have been known to choke to death when the collar gets caught on the crate. But with an adult dog who's very strong, particularly one who has demonstrated aggressiveness to other dogs, a choke collar will certainly give you more

Reeses and Poko demonstrate why mutts excel at agility trials.

control and could prevent a dog fight disaster, particularly if you live in an area where many dogs are on the street and your dog is straining to get at them.

Advanced training

Once you've mastered the basics and you are ready for a challenge, your mutt is poised to consider competing in dog agility trials. Trials are a great way to show off a mutt's talents. Dog agility, the sport in which a handler must beat the clock while guiding a dog off-leash through an obstacle course of A-frames, seesaws, tunnels, hoop jumps, weave poles, and the like—all without touching the dog or the equipment—has taken off as a popular pastime. It's quickly becoming the fastest-growing dog sport, giving a wonderfully modern, democratic spin to the term "sporting dog," a previously elitist term reserved for purebreds that accompany hunters.

The "big three" of dog agility are the United States Dog Agility Association (USDAA) in Richardson, Texas; the North American Dog Agility Council (NADAC) in Cataldo, Idaho; and the AKC. Interestingly, while the first two—incidentally, the two oldest—welcome mixed-breed competitors, with judging based on performance rather than breeding, the AKC, a newcomer to the agility field, still (surprise!) discriminates on the basis of breeding, operating on the old segregationist country club rule of "no mutts allowed." Must be because they don't want their purebreds to be upstaged by all those talented curs! Contact NADAC and USDAA for more information (see appendix, page 246).

Why is agility so popular with mutts and mutt people? As a general rule, mutts excel at dog sports because they're exceptionally intelligent. And guardians of mixed-breed dogs, having adopted from shelters or taken in strays, tend to be highly dedicated and motivated people. The real basis of agility is developing dogs who have the confidence to go through any obstacle that you guide them through, and watching them make progress is really rewarding. Many dogs are fearful in the first class, but by week two or three they're running across obstacles after their guardians have gently encouraged them and rewarded them. The end result is a dog with increased confidence in himself and his ability—and a dog who's more trusting of his guardian. So besides being fun and a way to burn off a dog's excess energy, agility is also a terrific way to cement the bond between people and dogs.

To get started, attend basic agility classes, which

are offered all across the country. Go to www.apdt.com, the Web site of the Association of Pet Dog Trainers (APDT), which lists about four thousand trainers and what they offer. Trainers offer group classes or private instruction. Generally, when starting out, you'll want a group class. Agility is such a high-energy sport, and there's so much athleticism involved, that when you're just beginning you can't expect a dog to work straight for an hour. In a group class, you work for five minutes at a time, then you take a ten- or fifteen-minute break while everyone else takes their turn; then you go on to your second round, and so on.

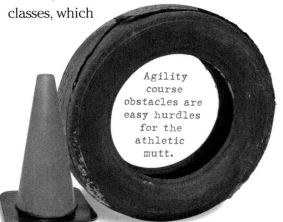

Agility course obstacles are easy hurdles for the athletic mutt.

Recommended Reading:
Basic Training

Fifty self-help books are no substitute for time with one real, live therapist. Similarly, dog-training books can't replace sessions with a real, live dog trainer. But they will help you get acquainted with the basics while you decide whether and when to take your mutt's training to a more advanced level. The following books, while not a substitute for a trainer, are especially good primers for training one-of-a-kind mutts because they respect each dog as an unique individual and emphasize positive reinforcement.

- ❏ The Power of Positive Dog Training by Pat Miller
- ❏ The Other End of the Leash by Patricia McConnell
- ❏ How to Be the Leader of the Pack by Patricia McConnell
- ❏ The Cautious Canine by Patricia McConnell
- ❏ Dogs Are from Neptune by Jean Donaldson
- ❏ The Culture Clash by Jean Donaldson
- ❏ Getting Started: Clicker Training for Dogs by Karen Pryor
- ❏ Don't Shoot the Dog! by Karen Pryor
- ❏ Dog-Friendly Dog Training by Andrea Arden

CLICK SCHTICK

While you locate a trainer in your area who uses positive methods, you can get off on the right foot working with your pet by using the clicker training method, a system for teaching behavior with positive reinforcement that was first used in the training of marine mammals and has since been used successfully on dogs, cats, horses, and birds. The Clicker Fun Kit for dogs (see appendix, page 247) includes everything you need to get started: an i-Click clicker, a pocket training guide, and the book Getting Started: Clicker Training for Dogs by clicker-training guru Karen Pryor.

bringing pup baby

by Rikke Brogaard

Often, parents feel nervous about the idea of bringing a new baby home to the dog. How will the dog respond? Will the baby be safe? Thousands of perfectly good dogs end up in shelters every year because people don't know there are some simple steps they can take. If your dog has shown aggression toward children before, or is a resource guarder (guarding food, people, and places), then contact an experienced positive dog trainer as soon as possible after you learn you are pregnant. The transition can be a smooth one, especially if your dog has never shown aggression toward kids. When I was pregnant, I had two rescued Great Danes who weren't necessarily kid-friendly. I worked a lot with the dogs throughout my pregnancy, and they ended up adoring my baby and thinking she was the greatest thing since the

Phoebe with her mutt, Totie.

invention of tennis balls. When it works, having children and dogs together is a beautiful thing. Here's how to make it work:

Brush up on basic good-manners training. If the dog jumps up when he greets people, teach him instead to sit politely and wait for attention. When he jumps, turn away and ignore him. He will probably jump more initially, maybe even bark, anything to get attention. When he finally gives up and sits down or even just stands with all four paws on the floor, turn to him, say *yes* in a happy voice, and give him a great treat. Keep working on this every time he goes to greet someone. Very soon, Fido will automatically sit and wait whenever anyone comes over.

Change causes stress in dogs, and stress can sometimes cause aggression, so avoid having everything in your mutt's life change when the baby arrives. Some things to work on before the arrival:

Sleeping: If your mutt is used to sharing your bed, and you'd like him to sleep somewhere else, give him a great, new bed way before the baby comes home. Help him transition to viewing his new bed as a favorite place by giving him irresistible treats or an exciting new toy the first time he lies down on it.

Walking schedule: If the mutt is used to a long walk every morning, begin breaking up the schedule months before the baby's arrival so the dog doesn't associate the baby with the end of all fun. Newborns keep irregular hours, so it's not realistic to expect you'll be able to stick to your mutt's exact schedule once the baby arrives. Before baby comes home, walk your mutt at different times of the day, have other people walk him, and mix up short and long outings so he gets accustomed to a more flexible schedule.

Make a point of having great things happen to the dog whenever the baby is in the room.

Attention and jealousy: If the dog is used to walking up to a human whenever he feels like it and nudging or barking until he gets attention, start ignoring this behavior completely (don't even say *no*; that counts as attention). When the dog finally gives up and lies down or does something else, leave him for about a minute, then walk over to him and lavish him with attention and praise. This will teach him that he'll get all the

attention he wants when he's calm and not pushy, and it puts you in control of when you want to interact with your mutt. When the baby comes home and friends and family come over to visit, always have someone give the dog attention, too.

Avoid trying to compensate in advance for the lack of time and attention the dog will receive. There's a tendency with new parents to feel guilty in advance and pay excessive attention to the dog right before the child arrives. Don't—it will only make the difference that much more drastic to the dog once the focus is off him. Remember that when people offer to help out with the new baby, that can mean taking your dog out for a walk. Have different family members and friends take turns walking and feeding the dog.

Meet the baby

When the baby arrives, the father should bring home a blanket from the hospital with the mother's and baby's scent on it before they come home. Let the dog smell the blanket and give him a delicious treat. Put the blanket in a plastic bag and seal it (to keep the smell). Take it out a few more times, have the dog sniff it, and give him a treat. The baby's scent combined with the familiar smell of the mother now has a positive association for the dog: Baby smell equals yummy treat.

During the first meeting, have someone other than the mom hold the baby. The dog probably hasn't seen the mother for a few days and will be very excited to see her. Let the mother give the dog a few minutes of attention before the dog is expected to meet the baby. Once the dog calms down a bit, have the father sit in a chair or on the couch with the baby, and have the dog approach on a leash. Most likely, he'll just smell her without touching her, and when he does, praise him and give him a treat.

Make a point of having great things happen to the dog whenever the baby is in the room. Baby appears, hot dogs do, too. Resist the urge to put the dog in another room when the baby is around. The dog can easily begin to resent the baby if, whenever she appears, he gets put aside. So be sure to make your mutt feel special. Don't give him attention only when the baby is asleep or away; you don't want your dog thinking "Baby gone equals happy time" and "Baby present equals dog feeling left out." You want him always associating the baby with happy times and feeling included.

The single most important thing I did was to walk quietly over to my dogs every day while they were sleeping and very gently grab an ear or a tail or a paw. When they woke up and looked confused, I had a great treat ready for them, right under their nose. I wanted, at all costs, to avoid ever having my child sneak up on them and grab them while they were sleeping, and having the dogs react—not unreasonably from a dog's perspective—by snapping or biting. To this day, my dogs think that being grabbed or pinched means free treats. Of course, never leave a child alone with a dog under any circumstances. But it's nice to know that you have a backup system for that one second when you're not looking.

Teaching children to respect dogs and be gentle with them is also important. Once your child is old enough, have her feed treats to your mutt often to strengthen the relationship between them.

Pepper the pit enjoys playtime with young Jack.

Best in Show Business

The most memorable movie stars are the players whose unique star quality breaks the mold. It follows that mutts, with one-of-a-kind looks, charm, and talents, are big-screen and Broadway naturals.

Movie Mutts

Benji (1974), directed by Joe Camp, launched a new cinematic era in mutts. Although mixed breeds had previously appeared on screen, only once before had a mongrel been a major player: in Charlie Chaplin's 1918 silent film *A Dog's Life*. Higgins, who played the original Benji, had crossed over from the small screen, having played the family dog on TV's *Petticoat Junction*. In 2004, Joe Camp opted for raw talent over an industry veteran, putting out a nationwide casting call and choosing an unknown shelter dog as the lead in *Benji Off the Leash*. Despite mutts' undeniable star quality, canine movie stars have primarily been purebreds, like Lassie, a collie, and Rin Tin Tin, a German shepherd.

Why has Hollywood favored purebreds over the people's dog? The reason is simple: With purebreds, it's easy to find body doubles to make the director's job easier. But locating two or more mutts that look alike enough to stand in for each other on a film set—or training a single mutt to do the work of two—requires time and patience, two things

> ## Why has Hollywood favored purebreds over the people's dog?

movie profession-
als have in short
supply. And most
filmmakers simply
don't believe that
one mutt can carry
an entire film. So
the movies have
given us purebreds
even when the
story called for
a mixed breed.
In William A.
Wellman's *The Call
of the Wild* (1935),
starring Clark Gable as author Jack
London, the sled dog Buck, the famous
mixed-breed narrator of London's novel,
was played by a purebred Saint Bernard
(go figure).

*Because
of Winn-Dixie*

Star quality

An early mutt reference
appears in *After the Thin Man* (1936).
Nick and Nora Charles return to San
Francisco with their beloved purebred
wirehaired fox terrier, Asta, in tow. Asta
is thrilled to be reunited with Mrs. Asta,

but his joy turns to dis-
may when he sees his
mate surrounded by
a litter of mutts. Poor
Asta had been cuck-
olded. For the most
part, mutts have
appeared in animated
features, where no
stand-ins are neces-
sary: the Disney classic
Lady and the Tramp
(1955); *All Dogs Go
to Heaven* (1989), in
which Burt Reynolds
provides the voice of Charlie, the leading mutt; and *Balto* (1995), in which
Kevin Bacon is the voice of the title
character, a heroic mixed-breed sled
dog who saves the children of Nome,
Alaska, from an epidemic of diphtheria
by bravely leading the sled team that
delivered medical supplies to them
in 1925.

The 2002 film *Road to Perdition* is
rich with haunting, painterly images, the
work of the late Conrad Hall, ASC, who
was awarded the Oscar posthumously
for Best Cinematography. The scenes that
portray young Michael Sullivan romping
with the dog on the beach are among

the most beautiful in this visually stunning movie. The production designers clearly went to great lengths to evoke the story's setting, 1920s Illinois, down to the automobiles and period furnishings. Only one detail didn't fit in this otherwise flawless celluloid tapestry: The dog cast as young Michael's best friend is a golden retriever, when he should have been (you guessed it) a mutt.

Like most gorgeous blondes, the golden in *Perdition* makes a powerful statement on screen without saying a word. But he's wrong for the part, and an anachronism in the context of the film. In the 1920s, goldens were quite rare in the United States—they weren't even recognized by the AKC until 1925. The right dog for the part would have been a pit bull mix. Tough looking on the outside but tender through and through, a pit mix would have meshed perfectly with Tom Hanks's portrayal of young Michael's father, a soulful gangster. What's more, in the early decades of the twentieth century, pit bulls and pit mixes were quite popular as family pets; in the 1930s, one would become a TV star as Petey of *Little Rascals* fame. Dog lovers look forward to a time when Hollywood pays closer attention to detail in canine casting, researching carefully which breeds and mixes were popular during which historical eras. The result would offer a

Ain't That a Bitch!

Pre-spay-neuter awareness, female dogs were blamed for being wanton and loose, and the "mongrel bitch" (in Shakespeare's phrase) was the object of great contempt. However, an early advocate of bitches' rights was Charlie Chaplin, whose costar in the 1918 silent film A Dog's Life is a mutt named Scraps. In the story, the Little Tramp rescues the mongrel bitch as she's being roughed up by a pack of fellow strays; the two underdogs become best friends and remain a team until the film's happy ending.

Chaplin with Scraps (left);
Petey with his Little Rascals

TIGHTROPE

Examining the 1984 movie thriller *Tightrope*, Kathie Coblentz, coeditor of *Clint Eastwood: Interviews*, detects and tracks what she calls "a subplot showing the superiority of mutts over purebreds." In the first scene, Clint Eastwood, playing Wes Block, a recently divorced cop with two young daughters, is on the trail of a killer. Block encounters a stray mutt and adopts the dog at his daughters' pleading, even though the family already has three (purebred) dogs. Later, the killer invades Wes's home, murdering his housekeeper and his three purebreds. The resourceful mutt is hiding in a closet, from which he emerges in time to intervene in a life-and-death struggle between Wes and the killer, whom he bites, thus enabling Wes to escape his stranglehold.

richer, more accurate visual pageant on screen.

On the subject of goldens and pit bulls, photographer-filmmaker Bruce Weber's most recent film, *A Letter to True* (2004), is a masterpiece. An impressionistic celebration of dogs, it naturally features plenty of footage of Weber's own five extremely photogenic golden retrievers, but it's really a love letter to all dogs, hard-luck mutts as well as pampered purebreds, and the people, both famous and anonymous, who dote on them all. Among the celebrities featured in the film is a pit bull mix named Dosha, a.k.a. "The Miracle Dog" (see page 120). Weber says that, after completing the film, he adopted his sixth dog: a rescued pit bull–Lab mix called Billie Holiday (see page 175). As if his feelings for the pretty black mutt weren't already evident in his choice of name (Weber is a serious jazz aficionado), it certainly shows in the

When Mickey Mouse arrived on the scene in 1928, he hung out with a handsome, coordinated dog named Pluto—and a homely, klutzy mutt named Goofy (whose original handle was Dippy Dawg). Blame it on Disney: Even today, many people describe their mixed-breed dogs as "goofy mutts."

FAMOUS MUTT

HEARTTHROB MUTT

The Magic Kingdom did mutts a great service in 1955, the birthday of a rakishly handsome mutt named Tramp, star of Lady and the Tramp. Tramp exhibits great savoir faire and bravery throughout the film, not to mention pasta-eating skills. At last, the mutt played the hero. His reputation resisted tarnish until The Last Days of Disco (1998), in which director and indie-film darling Whit Stillman uses Tramp, the beloved Disney mutt, as a scapegoat for contemporary relationship crises. The poor movie mongrel was subjected to hypercritical analysis by two verbose characters, one of whom argued that Tramp was merely a tool to "program women to adore jerks." Nice try. We're with Lady: Tramp's a dreamboat.

HERO MUTT

In 1964, Hanna-Barbera introduced a spoof of Superman called Underdog, featuring a canine caped crusader, his crush, Sweet Polly Purebred, and his buttoned-up alter ego, Shoeshine Boy. Years later, Hanna-Barbera undermined Underdog by introducing the villainous cartoon duo of Dick Dastardly and his lazy, scheming dog, Muttley, whose theme song went, in part, "Muttley, you snickering floppy-eared hound, / When courage is needed, you're never around!" Muttley was the quintessential "bad dog."

"I have five golden retrievers, and my sixth dog is a mix that we rescued in Florida," says photographer and jazz aficionado Bruce Weber. "Her name is Billie, for Billie Holiday, and she's part pit bull and part black Lab. This is my first time having a pit bull mix. I love her so much, and she's already become part of the family. She's black with beautiful white markings, and in the summer some of her hairs turn golden just like the retrievers. People are going to think I'm bleaching her, but I'm really not!"

—BRUCE WEBER

beautiful portrait he shot of Billie awaiting her close-up.

Shame on *Because of Winn-Dixie* (2005) for casting a purebred Berger de Picard (actually, several Bergers de Picard), an old French herding breed, as the movie's mixed-breed hero. Still, the casting works well enough because, like many old European purebreds, the Picard resembles an adorable mutt. Die-hard Mutt Mavens will want to stick with the award-winning book the movie was based on (see page 203).

Strays on stage

In 1976, Broadway director-lyricist Martin Charnin charged a young actor named William Berloni with the task of acquiring and training a dog to star as Sandy, the title character's canine sidekick in a new musical called *Annie*.

The now world-famous musical was based on the Depression-era comic strip *Little Orphan Annie,* which first appeared in the *Chicago Tribune* in 1924. In a 1925 strip, Annie rescues a pup being teased by a group of boys; the sandy-colored mutt repays the kindness over and over again, rescuing Annie from all sorts of rogues and ne'er-do-wells. Fittingly, Berloni cast a mutt from an animal shelter, the Connecticut Humane Society. "I was so horrified and moved by the appalling waste of canine talent I saw there," he recalls, "that I vowed to always rescue animals from shelters." After his success with Sandy, Berloni gave up acting to become Broadway's most sought-after animal trainer. The animals he's trained, of course, include a stable of Sandy mutts who've starred in various regional productions of *Annie* all over the country, thirty-two in all.

William Berloni, Broadway's go-to dog trainer, with Lola, one of his stable of beloved "Sandy" mutts.

Working Dogs

Grateful for their new leash on life, mutts enjoy giving back. The mutt's versatility, intelligence, and sensitivity make him a natural as a therapy dog or a service dog and an upstanding member of his community.

Boris, a mutt found abandoned in a Brooklyn dog run, is certified by three different organizations: Delta Society, Bide-A-Wee, and the Good Dog Foundation. He makes regular visits with his guardian, Alice Allay, to New York's Fort Tryon Nursing Home. Across the country, more and more therapy teams are volunteering their time at a wide range of hospitals and other care facilities.

According to the Americans with Disabilities Act, service dogs are dogs that have been "individually trained to do work or perform tasks for the benefit of a person with a disability." More and more organizations are recognizing that mutts can make brilliant assistance dogs, performing an astonishing variety of tasks, including alerting hearing-impaired people to sounds; responding when the handler has a seizure; assisting with mobility by acting as a disabled person's arms and legs, retrieving objects, and pulling wheelchairs; or offering psychiatric support.

Boris the therapy dog on one of his hospital visits. He looks so dapper in his official therapy dog vest that he's frequently greeted with "Que lindo!" (Spanish for "how handsome!").

Strangely, the duty of guiding the blind is still entrusted strictly to purebreds, but according to Assistance Dogs International, many hearing and other service dog programs use shelter dogs. Since most hearing dogs are rescued from shelters, most of them are mixed breeds. They come in all different sizes, shapes, and colors. They must be energetic, ready to work in an instant when a sound occurs. They must be friendly and people oriented. Organizations that accept mixed breeds into their training programs include Maryland's Fidos for Freedom; the Delta Society of Renton, Washington; People and Animals Who Serve (PAAWS) of Eugene, Oregon; Michigan's Paws With A Cause; and North Dakota's Great Plains Assistance Dogs Foundation, which trains alert dogs to help monitor people with different debilitating conditions, including seizure disorders, chronic heart disease, and diabetes. For more information, contact the Delta Society (www.deltasociety.org).

mobility
assistance
dog

LENDING A HELPING PAW

hearing dog

Hoss is a Scandinavian nickname for someone who's big and friendly.

Jennifer Weinik's study for a portrait of Hoss, an Oregon mutt certified in crisis response.

RECIPROCAL RESCUE

One morning in 2004, New Yorker Carina Schlesinger was playing fetch with her mutt, Cookie, in Central Park when she was attacked by a serial rapist with a knife. The man grabbed her by the hair, threw her to the ground, and pulled his pants down. Cookie, a shepherd mix, valiantly defended Schlesinger, attacking the would-be rapist despite his repeated attempts to kick the dog. Finally, the man let out a yelp and ran away. Police later arrested sex offender Tito Rodriguez; they were able to identify his DNA from the blood drawn by Cookie, which had stained Schlesinger's clothes. "My dog saved my life," Schlesinger said of her best friend, who was subsequently awarded a medal by North Shore Animal League (where she'd adopted him). "He's a good example of what can come out of a shelter."

NOTE BOOK

FROM HOBO TO HERO

Hoss, a shepherd mix certified by Oregon's Hope Crisis Response, was one of the therapy dogs who brought comfort to those who had lost family and loved ones in the attacks on the World Trade Center in 2001. Hoss is a Scandinavian nickname for someone who's big and friendly, which this Hoss is, as well as a reference to baseball legend Pepper Martin, a.k.a. "The Wild Hoss of the Osage," who had lived as a hobo before becoming second baseman for the St. Louis Cardinals' Gashouse Gang in the 1930s. This Hoss was a hobo, too; his people found him on the highway and later discovered he had been at the animal shelter twice before that.

Family Mutt

by Ally Sheedy

I first saw my mutt Geordie on a spring day in New York in 1990, the day after my birthday. I'd recently gotten together with the actor David Lansbury, who's now my husband, and we were walking around downtown when I saw a boy standing outside of a store with a solid-black, mixed-breed puppy. The dog was tiny, about six weeks old, and he had a chain tied around his little neck—that instantly got my attention. And for some reason, the boy was letting this adorable puppy walk through broken glass bottles. The whole thing really upset me, so I went over to the kid, trying to suss out whether or not the puppy had a good home. I said, "That's such a beautiful puppy!" The kid said, "Yeah, he is—you want him?" I asked him why he'd want to give away his puppy; he said, "I've had him for two weeks and I'm bored with him." The boy's mother came out of the store and asked for $100 to pay for the puppy's shots, which she had no proof that he'd even had. I remember David saying, "Are you crazy?" But I didn't care, I just wanted to rescue the dog. We brought the puppy home, fed him and bathed him, and took him to the vet to be dewormed; he was full of worms. We had to housebreak him, but he was really easy to train. One night Geordie turned around three times on our bed, then curled up and went to sleep. That was it—I was in love.

It took David a little bit longer—he'd never had a dog before—but when he fell for Geordie he *really* fell. That puppy became the love of David's life; the bond between them was so strong. They'd go for long walks and jogs in the park together, and David would hug Geordie and say, "My first doggie," like a little boy. Taking care of this puppy together cemented our relationship;

we immediately became a team. When you take a little dog who's all alone in the world and you completely commit to keeping him safe, caring for him, teaching him, respecting his fears and his needs, and earning his trust and his love, you realize it's very similar to having a kid. Animals are easier to take care of than children, but they demand equal amounts of commitment and love. All of a sudden there's all this new stuff you need to be aware of—like changing diapers!—because this little presence is there that wasn't before. With a dog, everything is much more compressed in terms of time, because dogs grow up more quickly. Raising Geordie definitely prepared us for parenthood. And when our daughter, Rebecca, was born in 1994, four years after we adopted Geordie, our little mutt still had some things to teach us about caring.

I wasn't one of those people who start looking for a home for their dog when a baby enters the picture; I think those people are idiotic. I wanted to learn the best way to integrate the baby with the dog, so I found an amazing

Rebecca

04 Dec 2000

THIs IS me And my momn And Jordie. I saw The BIg DiPer.

Rebecca Lansbury's tribute to her family mutt.

CRAYONS

CRAYONS

dog trainer, Shelby Marlowe. She recommended the minute we walk in with the newborn, to hold the baby at waist level and let Geordie sniff her. Don't ever make the dog leave the baby's room, Shelby said; let him go in there as much as he wants. Geordie was always mellow, so he was really gentle with the baby. He sniffed and licked her at first, and once she started crawling around, he'd sniff her little bottom as if she were a puppy. My daughter thought she was a dog. One day she even ate some kibble out of Geordie's bowl. I called the pediatrician in a panic, but she said not to worry, there were much worse things. While Rebecca was toddling around, Geordie would attach himself to her side and follow her wherever she went. His name was the first word she spoke; she pointed right at him and said, "Geordie!" When she could talk in whole sentences, Rebecca explained to me that she was "Little Blue Boy Pup." This went on for years, even after she realized she wasn't really a dog.

My daughter thought she was a dog.

Today, Rebecca is healthy, happy—and totally obsessed with animals. I think kids have a natural affinity for animals, and if you don't get in the way of that natural bonding, it's great for everyone. Animals really do help children learn how to be thoughtful and caring. In the last year of his life, Geordie fought a tough battle with colon cancer, and Rebecca was a wonderful caregiver. I was so proud of her: She was very gentle and patient with him. When he felt sick and cranky and wanted some space, she was mindful of his need for distance. And she was vigilant about his dietary restrictions—much more so than me! When I wanted to slip him a special treat, Rebecca reminded me that it would only make it harder for him to go to the bathroom later.

We're still not over Geordie's death. I still wake up expecting to find him curled up at my feet. Geordie was the constant in our life as a family—he started us on the family road.

The Homing Instinct

Some mutts just know how to take themselves out of bad situations and put themselves in situations where they'll meet a happy end.

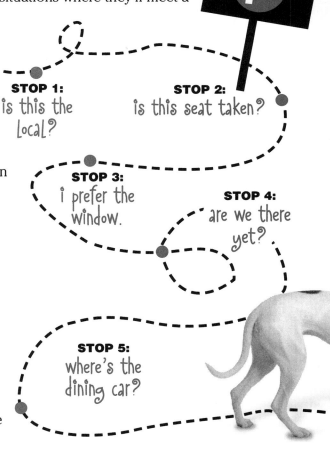

start ●

STOP 1:
is this the local?

STOP 2:
is this seat taken?

STOP 3:
i prefer the window.

STOP 4:
are we there yet?

STOP 5:
where's the dining car?

Consider Greystoke, a mutt found in New York's subway system at rush hour, wandering the F train platform in Brooklyn. A Good Samaritan collared the dog, took him to a vet, and assumed the cost for his care. He named him Greystoke, after the legend of Tarzan, "because he was scruffy but noble underneath." After a brief stay at a Brooklyn boarding kennel, Greystoke found a permanent home in Queens with author-screenwriter John Zmirak and his beagle Susie. Not long after Greystoke took his life-altering venture into New York's subterranean transit system, another canine commuter rode his way back to the home he'd been separated from.

On Christmas Eve, 2003, a retriever-spaniel mix took a solo ride on the Manhattan-bound Metro-North Commuter Railroad, boarding in Connecticut and landing at East 125th Street in Harlem. He earned himself the nickname Metro, plus several appearances on TV and in newspapers. But a microchip scan revealed the dog's real name was Brownie, and his original family lived in Maryland. It turned out that former owner Peggy Fulton had given the mutt away to a farming family when she adopted purebred puppies. The farming family in turn gave Brownie to their son-in-law, a truck driver, who took the dog with him on the road. But that lifestyle must not have appealed to the thirty-five-pound homebody mutt, because he ran away from the trucker in Connecticut and boarded the train for his famous homeward commute. So how did Brownie know to take the train that would head in precisely the correct southbound direction? Call it a mutt's built-in global pawsitioning system, which guides him to exactly where he wants to be.

In the summer of 2004, another canine commuter rode the rails, hopping on a No. 2 train in the Bronx and charming her fellow passengers. police officer John Santana collared the fare beater, took her to a city shelter, then returned the next day to adopt her.

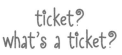

Greystoke, happy not to ride the rails.

ticket?
what's a ticket?

STOP 6:

STOP 7:
excuse me. getting off!

home

MUTT SHARE

For everything mutts learn from people, they have much to teach us, too. Mutt training is a two-way street: When people and mutts come together, the humans often learn and grow as much as the dogs. Mutts bring order, discipline, and a consistent schedule to human lives; they also impart a renewed sense of family, and they teach us, their people, to think outside the box. Exhibit A: Gracie and her humans, Perry Souchuk and Valerie Cihylik. You've heard of vacation home time-shares. Well, Souchuk and Cihylik share dog guardianship. The idea occurred to the Manhattan neighbors as they were bemoaning the fact that neither had time to devote to a dog—then a friend called and said there was a scrawny little puppy chained to a fence on East 18th Street. "Val and I went to meet her," says Souchuk. "She was a black Lab mix, and so cute! We figured it was meant to be." The newly minted canine co-owners took their charge to the vet for her first checkup. That was nine years ago. They've been happily splitting all dog responsibilities—including vet bills, food costs, and TLC—ever since. Gracie spends weekends with Souchuk and weekdays with Cihylik. Unorthodox it may be, but for some dog lovers, it's the best of both worlds. They get to enjoy canine companionship and unconditional love without the 24/7 responsibility.

Gracie the time-share mutt with her humans, Perry and Valerie.

La Dolce Vita
living with
and loving that mutt

dog /dawg/ n. "A kind of additional or subsidiary Deity designed to catch the overflow and surplus of the world's worship. This Divine Being in some of his smaller and silkier incarnations takes, in the affection of Woman, the place to which there is no human male aspirant."

--Ambrose Bierce, *The Devil's Dictionary*

Here's how
to spoil
'eM rotten.

Adopting a mutt changes that dog's life. In the process, many adopters make adjustments to their own lives to accommodate their new dog's needs. Of course, the concept of "need" is relative. A mutt's needs are simple: food, water, shelter, exercise, companionship, and veterinary care. Those basic requirements of dog guardianship haven't changed over the years. What has changed is people's desire to provide so much more.

With mutts who have endured hardship, there's the added desire to make up for lost time and missed pampering opportunities, not only for our own specific dogs, but also for all neglected underdogs. Maybe those who appreciate how far mutts have come through the centuries feel a need, if only symbolically, to alleviate the suffering of many by spoiling just one or two. We are spending money on dogs as never before. While other sectors of the economy have been hit hard in recent years, pet spending has seen consistent, healthy growth; it's in the billions of dollars, and rising all the time.

a mutt's needs are simple: food, water, shelter...

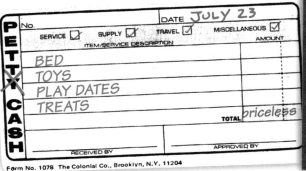

PETTY CASH

No.	DATE JULY 23		
SERVICE ☑	SUPPLY ☑	TRAVEL ☑	MISCELLANEOUS ☑
ITEM/SERVICE DESCRIPTION			AMOUNT
BED			
TOYS			
PLAY DATES			
TREATS			
		TOTAL	priceless
RECEIVED BY		APPROVED BY	

Form No. 1078 The Colonial Co., Brooklyn, N.Y. 11204

Trusty, ASPCA alumnus, likes his breakfast civilized.

Creature Comforts

Being around dogs has been scientifically proven to lower blood pressure and reduce the risk of heart disease; obviously, we're repaying the myriad ways that dogs improve our lives by spending big so they can live large. Considering how the mutt's life has historically been valued cheaply, if at all, it's especially satisfying to see instances of underdogs enjoying a lifestyle that's the envy of their purebred counterparts.

before

after

Mutt people are happy to include their beloved dogs in every aspect of their wildly different lifestyles, and the mutts are loving every minute of that quality time. Inclusion was all they ever wanted, going all the way back to the primordial, prehistoric mutt.

Leave it to the mixed-breed dog: Like the hero of F. Scott Fitzgerald's *The Great Gatsby,* he can be counted on to make a smooth transition from unnoticed nobody to admired, envied, worshipped canine deity. He moves with ease from the animal shelter to the living room posh enough to be featured in a shelter magazine. In every way imaginable, he fulfills his uniquely American destiny of self-invention and reinvention. And in continually striving to improve his own lot in life, he enriches the lives of all those who love him.

And so to bed

Believe it or not, a dog bed is not a luxury; it's a necessity. Dogs sleep twelve to sixteen hours daily. And even if your mutt shares your bed, you'll need to provide him with a place of his own to retreat to when he wants space. It's easy to spend four, even five, figures on a designer dog bed. But that's not necessary, and it won't guarantee a good night's sleep. Options range from the most basic—a simple slice of polyurethane foam with a removable, washable cover—all the way to a high-quality upholstered piece of real furniture designed just for dogs. The price tags range from $20 to $20,000. I recommend a cushion that won't flatten like a pancake in two months, stuffed with polyester fiberfill, and topped off with a cover that's not only removable and washable, but also stylish enough to coordinate with your furniture so you won't mind having it around. Avoid

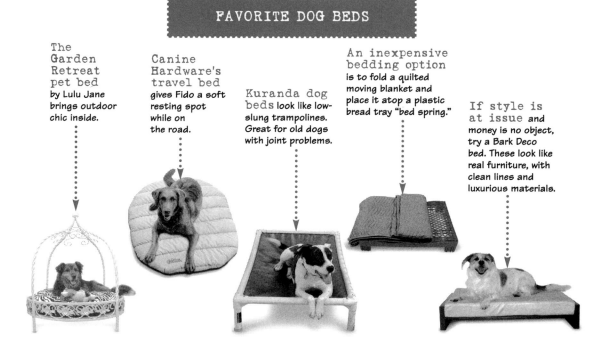

FAVORITE DOG BEDS

The **Garden Retreat pet bed** by Lulu Jane brings outdoor chic inside.

Canine Hardware's travel bed gives Fido a soft resting spot while on the road.

Kuranda dog beds look like low-slung trampolines. Great for old dogs with joint problems.

An inexpensive bedding option is to fold a quilted moving blanket and place it atop a plastic bread tray "bed spring."

If style is at issue and money is no object, try a Bark Deco bed. These look like real furniture, with clean lines and luxurious materials.

feather fillings because, just like people, some dogs are allergic. Beds come in all shapes. Most dogs don't care about the shape. They just need the bed to be big enough to turn around in several times before they settle in, and most dogs prefer a defined edge. Look for a bed that has a walled construction, not just a pillow. Mutts like something that lifts them up off the floor, makes them feel snug, and gives them a place to rest their chins.

Quilted moving blankets provide an inexpensive sleeping option with the important virtue of versatility. Folded and placed on the floor, they form a cozy nest that dogs can arrange and customize for themselves; spread across your bed, they double as a durable bedspread to

Dogs know how to customize blankets to make their own comfortable nesting spots, as this double portrait of Daisy, by artist Martha Szabo, shows.

. . . in continually striving to improve his own lot in life, he enriches the lives of all those who love him.

protect fine linens from the depredations of paws that have walked the mean city streets. For dogs who prefer to be up off the floor, simply fold up one moving blanket and place it on top of an inverted plastic bread tray, which serves as a comfy canine box spring and is big enough to support my medium-to-large mutts. For a higher-tech, more expensive version, check out Kuranda dog beds, a hammocklike bed suspended from a durable metal frame. And for the ultimate in designer dog bedding, there's Eloise Inc., makers of gorgeous cushions featured at the dog-friendly Starwood Hotels (see appendix, page 247), or moisture-shedding beds by Crypton Super Fabrics (page 249).

Mutts in toyland

Some mutts have so many toys, they require a toy chest to corral them all. Toys are more than just playthings; keeping canine boredom at bay significantly extends the life of home furnishings. So think of dog toys as furniture insurance, keeping jaws, paws, and claws gainfully employed so they won't feel compelled to apply themselves to your favorite belongings.

Some mutts will be thrilled to chase and retrieve balls and tear into chew toys; others will appear bewildered in the face of playthings, no matter how shiny and happy the toy. This is because many rescued dogs grow up without the luxury of games and toys, and while some can catch on that they're fun, others simply can't be bothered with what they appear to dismiss as "stupid pet tricks." This does not mean there's anything wrong with your mutt; he's not defective because he doesn't love to play, he's just exhibiting an opinion—and being opinionated is a unique aspect of muttness to be prized.

Not all dogs will love the tried-and-true playthings listed opposite, but I've yet to meet the mutt who doesn't adore gnawing on raw bones from the butcher or organic-meat supplier. These are generally quite inexpensive (beef bones average about a dollar a pound, organic parts about three dollars a pound) and keep a mutt occupied for hours. Just remember that bones leave behind a spectacular mess, so confine your mutt and his raw bone to an area of your home that has no upholstered

I've yet to meet the mutt who doesn't adore gnawing on raw bones.

THE MUTT TOY CHEST

sterilized marrow bones:
available at pet stores, these are white and have a hollow into which you can put peanut butter or cheese

tirebiter:
these are made from recycled car tires for environmentally friendly fun

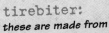

kong:
power chew toy made of rubber; smear inside with a small amount of peanut butter, cheese, or liverwurst

squeaky toys:
either latex or plush, like the Cheeky Squeaky (left)

tennis balls:
(round or cube-shaped) plus a Chuckit! to help you toss the ball

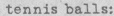

dental bone:
to keep teeth clean (the Greenies brand is ubiquitous but has been known to cause choking and diarrhea); Breath-A-Licious (right), which contains chlorophyll, mint, and parsley, is the best and safest option

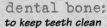

frisbee:
ideal if your mutt is part border collie; should be soft, like the Animal Planet Toss a Turtle by Premier Pet or Chuckit! Flying Squirrel, so as not to damage a mutt's teeth

furniture and a floor surface that's easy to clean (i.e., the kitchen or porch). And please don't ever cook the bones, as they can splinter and lodge in your mutt's intestinal tract. Always serve bones raw. If you have a multimutt household, avoid potential fights by separating your dogs prior to distributing bones.

House-proud mutt people prefer that their dogs' toys look aesthetically pleasing, especially if they must be strewn all over the living-room floor. (Incidentally, one very stylish way to corral errant toys is to house them in an attractive Lucite cube, which coordinates with most furnishing styles and permits easy viewing of toys.) These people have no problem spending extra to ensure that their dogs' toys combine function with style. The manufacturers producing the best-looking performance dog toys on the market are Bettie, Bodhi Toys, George San Francisco, Orbee, and Wagwear. If your mutt has the annoying habit of chewing your eyeglasses when you're not looking, try l.a.Eyeworks' prescription for this common problem: a chew toy made to look like a pair of chic specs. Pairs come in pink, green, or sky blue.

TOYS TO AVOID

Rawhide in any shape or form, or any preserved animal part, such as ears, hooves, or testicles. Dogs work themselves into a frenzy when attacking these prehistoric reminders of the kill—not good. Besides packing pounds on your dog, these high-fat items, when ingested too quickly, can cause choking or intestinal blockages; can carry salmonella bacteria and contribute to gastric torsion (bloat); and often promote aggressive behavior as dogs jealously guard them against other dogs and people in crazed, Daffy Duck–like displays. Try Snooks Sweet Potato Dog Chews, a natural, digestible alternative to rawhide made from organic sweet potatoes, or veggie "Piggears" made of wheat.

Fuzzy little stuffed animals. Biting off small parts can cause intestinal blockages; plus, if there are babies and small children in the house, the dog will have trouble distinguishing between his own and the kids' toys. Bad.

Fashion Hounds

The **accessory basics** are the same for mutts as they are for any other dog. As for clothing, mutts technically don't have wardrobe needs, but if their own coats are short, they do appreciate an extra layer of warmth in inclement weather.

Leashes & collars

The **first wardrobe element every mutt needs is a leash.** The sliplead, which is a lasso that incorporates a collar and leash, is an option for emergencies or temporary use. It's best to have a separate collar and leash. Some mutts have experienced neck trauma in their previous life and dislike neck tension. They might make choking sounds when they use a collar and leash. For those dogs, a harness is a good option. However, if your mutt is big and strong, a harness will increase his pulling power. Go with the Softouch SENSE-ation harness, which sits low on the shoulders and discourages pulling.

A leash can be made of anything you, the dog walker, doesn't mind handling: leather, nylon, or canvas. (This is about you, not the dog.) Look for something that won't chafe your hand. Many leashes come with foam handles that make them a pleasure to hold (if not to behold).

The collar, on the other hand, is about your dog's comfort. Some short-coated mixes find nylon webbing very irritating. It can actually rub the hair off the neck, resulting in a rash. For those dogs, leather, canvas, or a lightweight metal chain is the best option. (Metal collars should always be removed in the house; a dog can wear leather and nylon indoors and out.)

Chew on This:
Thanks to my mutt Pici, who used to have a charming habit of gnawing her collar right off her own neck, Lupine collars have a special place in my heart. The company offers a lifetime guarantee: Should anything happen to damage your Lupine collar—yes, including chewing—mail it back, and they'll send you a replacement.

> "Safety orange and military green are the perfect boy-dog colors, for an urban guerilla dog look!"

wear one. Burberry even makes a four-legged version of its iconic trench; Land's End offers the canine equivalent of its popular Squall Jacket. The most comfortable rainwear is a neoprene vest made by Cabela's, a mail-order hunting supplier. Whether or not you favor the sport of hunting, your mutt can benefit from gear designed for hunting dogs. Hunters care about their retrievers and pointers, and they've created a demand for functional, well-engineered canine protective gear. I've tried every possible sweater and coat on my large mutts; in cold, wet weather the best solution, as Cabela's knows, is a vest made of neoprene, the fabric

Sweaters

In winter, short-coated mutts need an extra thermal layer, especially on freezing late-night and early-morning walks. Shaggy, long-coated mutts like chow mixes or border collie mixes are naturally dressed for the weather. Dogs who refuse to walk outside in the rain might be more inclined to do so if they are wearing a raincoat. Canine raincoats are a smart and practical fashion accessory if you can convince your dog to

used to make scuba suits. Wool sweaters are fine when the weather is dry, but when it snows, the sweater gets

Chinoiserie says "canine chic."

FOUR-LEGGED FASHION

These are a few of my favorite places to buy dog clothing and accessories.

Trixie + Peanut. A great Web site for all your canine fashion needs. (www.trixieandpeanut.com)

Cabela's. Great collars, in brilliant safety orange, with identification tags riveted to the collar (to avoid that annoying jangling noise made when ID tags collide with dog collar hardware). Cabela's neoprene vests are just the thing for big dogs to wear in a downpour. (www.cabelas.com)

Wagwear. Excellent leashes that coordinate well with orange collars; they're olive drab with a safety orange stripe. And if you don't believe that this is the height of chic, take it from designer John Bartlett: "Safety orange and military green are the perfect boy-dog colors, for an urban guerilla dog look!" (www.wagwear.com)

Fab Dog. Fashion-forward collars, leashes, toys, and more. Does your dog need a bathrobe? Probably not, but it's super cute. (www.fab-dog.com)

Eloise Inc. In addition to dog beds, this firm carries rhinestone-studded collars and other swank accoutrements. (www.eloiseinc.com)

Ella Dish. For the preppy pooch, collars made with striped grosgrain ribbon. (www.elladish.com)

George. No-nonsense dog gear that's as pretty as it is practical. (www.georgesf.com)

Orvis. For large breeds, this Lab-loving company offers a dashing fleece turtleneck pullover that's simply fetching. (www.orvis.com)

Woozie Wear. If you want knitwear to match your mutt, this is the place to go. (www.madisonavenuedog.com/wooziewear.html)

Land's End. The makers of the classic Squall Jacket now offer a sporty canine version. (www.landsend.com)

THE FORGOTTEN DOG

You'll quickly discover when you go shopping for Fifi that, just as with high fashion for humans, designers seem to cater only to petite creatures. You'll pick up an adorable little four-sleeved cashmere sweater, say, but when you look for Large, you find they don't make it. What's a big-boned mutt to do? You can check back with the retailers, because some of them are becoming hip to this emerging market. Or you can always learn to knit.

uncomfortably wet and heavy (and dogs don't like the scratchy feeling of wool). Plus, neoprene vests come in very cool camouflage patterns as well as always-appropriate—and chic—safety orange.

Footwear

In the winter in urban and sub-urban areas, sidewalks and streets are covered with an ice-melting salt that is corrosive to canine paw pads, causing burns on the feet and internal damage when a dog licks his paws. To prevent this, put booties on your dog. If your dog refuses to wear them, try Musher's Secret instead. Musher's Secret is a paw pad salve formulated for sled dogs that forms a barrier between the skin and the salt. Remember to wipe your dog's paw pads when you return home so they don't leave a greasy mess. If you yourself use salt in the winter, consider switching to Safe Paw Ice Melter. This is the salt used at airports and nuclear power plants—places that really can't tolerate corrosion—and it works.

MUTT HABERDASHERY

leash

outerwear

footwear

dapper dog

COSTUME PARTY

Costume accessories are fine once a year, on Halloween or for occasional photo ops (I myself have been guilty of putting reindeer antlers on a pit bull), but dressing a dog in a costume every day is ridiculous—especially if the dog already has a full coat and might be uncomfortable wearing an outfit. Please have some compassion for our littlest fashion victims, who have no voice to protest. Just say no to daily doses of mini motorcycle jackets, tuxedos, tiaras, and the like.

Pepper

I required Pepper to tolerate reindeer antlers for the duration of this photo op, and not one minute longer.

Gringo

Some habits are hard to break. As the renowned photographer Mary Ellen Mark proves with this portrait of Gringo, a dog she rescued in Mexico and re-homed, few subjects are more compelling than a mutt in costume.

Mutt Lit:
a Mixed breed reading list

If you are a mutt enthusiast, you'll want to read the canon of great mongrel literature. Mutts have been derided throughout history, true. But they have been lauded, too, in works great and small. Here is my list of the notable books on these noble creatures.

Beautiful Joe: An Autobiography by Marshall Saunders, pen name of Margaret Marshall Saunders (1893). The canine version of *Black Beauty*, this is the first novel to be written from the point of view of a mutt, specifically a pit bull (back then they were called bull terriers) who is rescued from terrible abuse and adopted by a loving family. Not the greatest work of literature, but historically important for its message and as an early chronicle of the American animal-rights movement.

The Call of the Wild by Jack London (1903). Widely regarded as London's masterpiece, this is the story of Buck, a Saint Bernard mix, told from Buck's point of view, following him as he is stolen from his comfortable California home, then sold into slavery as a sled dog in the Alaskan Klondike.

Patch: The Story of a Mongrel by Moyra Charlton (1931). A precociously literary teen, Charlton penned this sweet tale of a lost terrier mix seeking a reunion with his boy.

All Dogs Go to Heaven by Beth Brown (1943). This Faustian tale of a criminally minded mutt named Hobo, who comes back to Earth and is redeemed by making the ultimate sacrifice for a little girl, was retold and Hollywoodized in 1989 as an animated movie voiced by Burt Reynolds (stick with the book).

The Collected Stories of Jean Stafford by Jean Stafford (1992). There are some writers so great that they make other writers throw up their hands in despair; Stafford is one such writer. Included in this collection is her dazzling story "In the Zoo," which first appeared in *The New Yorker* in 1953; in it, the struggle for the soul of a mutt named Laddy occupies center stage.

My Dog Tulip by J. R. Ackerley (1956). In his brilliant, controversial memoir about life with his beloved rescued Alsatian (that's Queen's English for German shepherd), Ackerley searches for a "husband" for Tulip and eventually locates one— "a disreputable, dirty mongrel, Dusty by

name, in whom Scottish sheep-dog predominated"—so that purebred Tulip gives birth to a litter of mixed-breed pups, despite the author having precious little food due to wartime privations.

Old Yeller by Fred Gipson (1956). In Texas, fourteen-year-old Travis experiences hate at first sight upon meeting a stray dog (Yeller refers at once to the color of the mutt's coat and the quality of his bark), then soon grows to love him. Heartbreak ensues when Yeller is bitten by a rabid wolf and Travis must put his loyal dog out of pain with a swift gunshot. Kleenex is a must; you'll be crying by the third sentence.

Ribsy by Beverly Cleary (1964). When one family's mutt, Ribsy (so named because his ribs were sticking out when he was chosen at the pound), gets in the wrong station wagon at the shopping center parking lot, there begins a series of adventures as he desperately searches to rejoin his family. (Ribsy first appears in Cleary's 1950 book

The statue of Ribsy the mutt draws human and canine admirers to Cleary Park in Portland, Oregon.

Henry Huggins, and there's a statue of the mutt in Cleary Park in Portland, Oregon.)

Vic and Blood by Harlan Ellison (1968). The sci-fi master's tale of a young man and his telepathic mongrel, who struggle to survive in the aftermath of nuclear war, was made into the so-bad-it's-great 1975 movie *A Boy and His Dog,* starring Don Johnson, Jason Robards, and the mutt who played Tiger on *The Brady Bunch.*

Sounder by William H. Armstrong (1970). This Newbery Award–winning novel for young adults is set in the Depression-era American South. When the father of a sharecropper family is taken to jail, the family dog, Sounder— a coon dog mix, best friend to the share-cropper's eldest son, and the only character in the story to be given a name— is shot and disappears while protecting his master. Sounder eventually returns, crippled and emaciated—a symbol of the family's resilience in the face of hardship.

King: A Street Story by John Berger (1999). A dog named King, who lives with a group of homeless people in the shadow of a motorway, is the narrator of this story of displacement and loyalty by a Booker Prize–winning novelist: "All dogs dream of forests, whether they've ever been in one or not. Even Egyptian dogs dream of forests."

The Dog Who Rescues Cats: The True Story of Ginny by Philip Gonzalez (1996). In his sweet memoir, Gonzalez introduced the world to his now-famous rescued mutt Ginny, who spends her time selflessly rescuing and caring for felines in distress.

Timbuktu by Paul Auster (2000). Auster's moving tale of homelessness is told from the point of view of Mr. Bones, "a mutt of no particular worth or distinction." After the death of his master, Willy G. Christmas, Mr. Bones muses on the afterlife, the place Willy had called Timbuktu.

Sweetie: From the Gutter to the Runway by Mark Welsh (2001). The soufflé-light story of Sweetie's metamorphosis from near-roadkill to fashion-world celebrity, complete with her Diana Vreeland-worthy dictums ("I'm that rare woman of color who is black, white, and brown"), did much to bring fashionistas around to the idea that mixed breeds are bone-chic.

Because of Winn-Dixie by Kate DiCamillo (2001). In this Newbery Honor Book, a ten-year-old girl named Opal has much to learn from her happy mutt, Winn-Dixie.

The Stray Dog by Marc Simont (2001). While out on a picnic, a family meets a little lost mutt named Willy. Based on a true story by Reiko Sassa, this Caldecott Honor Book for young readers is required reading if you're raising kids to be mutt lovers.

Flawed Dogs: The Year-End Leftovers at the Piddleton "Last Chance" Dog Pound by Berkeley Breathed (2003). In this book, Breathed, the Pulitzer Prize–winning cartoonist and creator of the character Opus, celebrates pound hounds: "The bent and plain, / The unbalanced bod, / The imperfect people / And differently pawed."

Getting Lucky by Susan Marino (2005) and **Miracle Dog** by Randy Grim (2005). The subjects of both true stories cheated death, becoming spokesmutts for shelter animals.

Muttropolitan Home

Leaving his toys all over the place is just one of the ways a mutt will influence your home decor. More than any other dog "breed," the mutt knows how to trade up from a life on the streets to the lush life, so prepare to share your sofa. For the dogs, it's not just about luxury. Mutts really want to be with us, and the more aspects of our lifestyle we share with them, the happier they—and ultimately we—will be.

If you do intend to share your fine furnishings with your mutt, there are several ways to ensure that your interior will always look its best. Performance furnishings are a must in a home with mutts (or any home that's ready to welcome any animal or human, especially children). That means sofas and chairs should be slipcovered or upholstered in animal-friendly fabrics. Leather and vinyl are excellent choices for homes with animals (of course, vinyl cleans up easier than leather). Two excellent fabrics are Ultrasuede, a polyester microfiber that looks and feels like suede but is machine washable and spot cleanable, and Chella, a synthetic chenille that is also machine washable. Groundworks, a division of the fabric giant Lee Jofa, makes a collection of indoor-outdoor upholstery fabrics that are as soft to the touch as they are strong. Velese by Crypton Super Fabric is another extremely durable and stylish option; it's soft to the touch, yet liquids roll off it. These brands are not inexpensive, but they perform beautifully and come in a wide range of colors and patterns designed to coordinate with a variety of different decorating styles (for sources, see appendix, page 249).

If changing your upholstery fabric is not in the cards now, you can explore the slipcover option. The best fabric for slipcovers is machine-washable cotton or linen. Many furniture manufacturers offer sofas and chairs with removable, washable slipcovers; when ordering furniture from, say, Crate & Barrel, ask about purchasing a second set of slipcovers. Sure Fit slipcovers are an easy, off-the-rack option, but if your furniture has a distinctive shape, you'll need to investigate custom slipcovers. Launder slipcovers once a week to keep them looking their best; allow them to air dry (so they don't shrink or fade); and keep at least one extra set on hand in case an accident necessitates a quick change.

If slipcovering is not an option, you can use positive reinforcement to train your mutt to nest in his very own chair—preferably an old one you don't care about. Praise him lavishly and give him treats when he sits or sleeps on that chair.

In homes with animals who are elderly or ailing, there are bound to be accidents. If you don't want to limit your dog's access to the furniture, consider a clear vinyl covering (see appendix, page 249). Of course, design professionals dismiss it as tacky, but there are creative ways to live stylishly with clear vinyl. As long as you order clear slipcovers with clear piping (never gold or silver piping), as I did, you can't be busted by the style police. The advantage of clear plastic slipcovers is that you can stuff them with anything soft and colorful that catches your fancy, from skeins of thick yarn to cushions covered in some intriguing, precious silk fabric that no one in their right mind would expose to

Train your mutt to nest in his very own chair.

everyday use without a protective barrier. Another option is to have your upholsterer attach clear vinyl directly to the piece of furniture, instead of slipcovering. For my room in the 2003 DogHaus designer showhouse, I had my upholsterer, J & P Decorators of Long Island City, New York, pad the seat and back of two antique shield-back chairs, then cover them with Velvetaire, attaching the vinyl to the chair frame with elegant brass tacks. The result raised the much-maligned clear vinyl to grand new aesthetic heights.

Mutt fanciers enjoy thinking up creative new ways to give dogs easy, convenient access to the best seats in the house. Many mutts need a leg up, especially elderly and arthritic dogs, so their people

Saylor the mutt is the inspiration behind k. d. lang's song "Curiosity." Lang decorated her home in earth tones to camouflage Saylor's wet pawprints. "We go swimming together a lot in the ocean," she explains. "We're very fond of each other."

are building custom-made step-ups, covering them in skidproof materials so the dogs won't slip and injure themselves. For those who aren't handy with carpentry, enterprising companies are offering ready-made products to assist dogs in reaching our beds, sofas, window ledges, and automobiles. The Scamp Ramp is a high-density foam ramp that supports up to eighty-five pounds; its interchangeable covers look ready for their close-up in *Metropolitan Home.*

THE WRITING ON THE WALL

Recognizing that flaunting mutt pride can be extremely decorative, the wallpaper firm Tyler Hall recently unveiled Dennis Lee's new design called "Adopt Me," featuring charming renderings of mixed-breed dogs in a pattern that—like a mutt—is equally at home in a wide range of stylish interiors.

DOG BOWLS

Mutts can leave their style imprint on every room of your home. Why shouldn't your mutt's bowls be as stylish as your tableware? Fiesta and Bauer, makers of colorful, highly collectible pottery, both make great-looking dog bowls that coordinate with the best-dressed dining tables. And for those who prefer the durability of stainless-steel bowls but don't love the industrial look of metal, Prima Pet offers metal bowls in a range of bright colors, with a black rubber ring around the bottom to prevent sliding.

Besides upholstery, there are a few other basic rules to keep top of mind when designing a mutt-friendly home. Avoid wool rugs, which are magnets for hair and dust, not to mention accidents. All animals have a way of selecting the middle of, say, an expensive Tibetan carpet as the ideal place to throw up. Also, it's not uncommon for dogs to urinate on a wool carpet, as the natural lanolin in the fibers makes the rug smell like sheep. To your dog, that's another animal invading his territory, so his natural response is to pee on it. Shag rugs, or any floor covering with a deep pile, are open invitations to dig and chew, and they should be avoided. Long fibers, if ingested, can

cause fatal intestinal blockages. The best flooring in an animal-friendly house is anything that's easy to mop clean: bare wood, tile, or vinyl. Thankfully, vinyl flooring—as oft-maligned by decorators as clear vinyl slipcovers—is now available in bright, stylish colors and patterns thanks to a company called Lonseal.

If you insist upon a rug but want a low-maintenance one, check out the rubber-backed synthetic rugs from IKEA (many of these are machine washable and come in dazzling colors and patterns) or modular carpet tiles by Interface FLOR. When an accident happens, simply remove the affected carpet tiles, discard, and replace them with identical ones—brilliant.

What's on the walls is also important. Be sure to use a paint finish that is easy to wipe clean, as dogs have a way of coming off on the walls (the oils in their coats, when rubbed against the walls, can quickly gray a coat of white paint). That has traditionally meant covering walls with satin or eggshell finish, which is not the decorator's choice. But now fans of flat paint have the option of using Matte by Benjamin Moore, which can be wiped clean (for resources, see appendix, page 250.)

What if you meet your mutt match while you're single, then you hook up with the human of your dreams, only to discover that he or she is allergic to dogs? There's no dilemma: To keep your mutt and your mate, there are simple ways to ease allergy discomfort:

4 Buy a HEPA air filter to help minimize airborne allergens.

6 Be strict about keeping pets out of the bedroom at all times (close the door), and shed all clothing before entering the bedroom, so you don't carry allergens in with you.

2 Acquire a powerful vacuum cleaner such as the Dyson DC14 Animal (available at Target stores), designed to pick up pet particles. Eliminate wall-to-wall carpeting and area rugs, which trap allergens and are tough to clean; opt for bare wood, tile, or vinyl floors.

5 If the air is dry, pets will shed more and release more dander. Keep the air moist with a low-tech humidifier: Fill a small pot with water and set it on top of the radiator to create steam.

1 Wipe Spot's coat once weekly with a product called Petal Cleanse, a gentle, all-natural cleanser-moisturizer that removes dander, saliva, and urine (to order, go to www.allergic2pets.com).

3 Avoid fabric draperies, which are magnets for allergens. Instead, get window shades and blinds. The best ones are paper Redi Shades, which are inexpensive enough that you can simply toss them when they become too dirty.

7 If all else fails, consult an allergy specialist.

Fine Arf

Every year, in February, the Manhattan auction house Doyle New York teams up with the London auction house Bonhams to present "Dogs in Art," a sale of dog-themed paintings.

The event is timed to coincide with the Westminster Kennel Club Dog Show, which takes place across town at Madison Square Garden at the same time. And not surprisingly, the majority of the mostly nineteenth- and twentieth-century paintings, sculptures, and other items for sale depict purebred dogs,

Left and right: For artist Elizabeth Peyton, her mutt Harry is a favorite subject.

usually show-ring champions. But today's mutt aficionados are according their beloved mixed breeds the same artistic consideration previously restricted to pedigreed dogs and aristocratic humans, commissioning museum-quality mutt representations in every possible medium—painting, sculpture, photography, and silhouette cutting— to immortalize their too-long-underrepresented dogs. Highly respected photographers, Mary Ellen Mark, Bruce Weber, and Sebastião Salgado among them, are turning their lenses on mutts and strays.

Sculptor Jennifer Weinik's life-size bronze bust of my dog Sam.

Modern Mutts

More and more, contemporary artists are incorporating images of mutts in narrative paintings, where the dogs' presence adds powerful symbolic resonance. Not surprisingly, many of these artists have mutts themselves. Painter Elizabeth Peyton's work has been exhibited in the prestigious Whitney Museum Biennial. Her painting *Richard and Harry* depicts her mutt nestling in the lap of her fellow artist Richard Prince,

Jasper as re-created by his human, the artist Patricia Cronin.

with the dog's chew bone prominent in the foreground. "I paint Harry often," Peyton says. "Richard had come over to a party at our house, and Harry had never met him, but after Richard sat down Harry climbed on the couch and went to sleep in his lap. I was touched by how comfortable and happy they seemed with each other."

Proclaiming the mixed breed's right to artistic immortality, mutt people are busy rewriting the history of dogs in art. In Philadelphia, sculptor Jennifer Weinik creates astonishingly detailed, life-size bronze portraits of mutts in a style reminiscent of Auguste Rodin. In 2003, New York artist

. . . and the life-size sculpture modeled in his image by Jennifer Weinik.

Patricia Cronin made headlines with *Memorial to a Marriage,* her larger-than-life-size mortuary sculpture executed using computerized carving technology. A portrait of herself and partner Deborah Kass reclining in tender embrace, the marble monument is on view in New York's Woodlawn Cemetery, over what will be the couple's final resting place. Their beloved schnauzer-poodle mix Jasper predeceased them, so Cronin created a clay model as a study for her next marble mortuary sculpture: a memorial to her mutt.

"I am a total mutt enthusiast," says artist Kenny Scharf of Los Angeles, who has three: Beiju (Portuguese for "kiss"), a pit bull mix; Baby, a Chihuahua-dachshund cross; and Winston, a Chihuahua-pug. "I always tell people to get dogs from shelters or from the street. Why go to a breeder?" All three appear in Scharf's monumental painting *Family Portrait*, a moving tableau in which Scharf's mutts, past and present, occupy pride of place alongside all the other important members of his family, forebears as well as offspring. The mutts are family, too. Meanwhile, in New York, Roy Kortick's painting *K with Unicorn* depicts the artist's mutt, a pit bull mix named K, superimposing her figure with images from the fifteenth-century Unicorn Tapestries.

MUTT MONUMENT:
Semper fido

Tokyo's Shibuya train station is the site of a famous monument to Hachiko, the purebred Akita who waited at the station faithfully for his beloved human, Professor Ueno, to return from work every day for nine years after the professor died of a stroke at the office in 1925. America's answer to Hachiko is a mutt named Shep, who began a vigil at the Fort Benton, Montana, train station in 1936, after watching the casket of his beloved human loaded onto an eastbound train. Legend has it that the man Shep waited for was a sheepherder named Ray Castle, but according to the Montana Historical Society, there's no hard evidence to back this up. What we know for sure is that Shep took up residence at the station, hopefully scanning the crowds of passengers on the platform, until his death in 1942 (he was hit by a train). He got a hero's funeral, at which taps were sounded. In 1994, a monumental statue was erected in Shep's honor; it was created by the late Bob Scriver, who also sculpted the monument to legendary showman William "Buffalo Bill" Cody in Cody, Wyoming.

Mutts & the city

Long before *Sex and the City* catapulted her to worldwide acclaim, actress Sarah Jessica Parker received some of the best reviews of her career back in 1995, when she starred off Broadway in A. R. Gurney's play *Sylvia* about a man who disrupts his marriage by bringing home a stray dog. And what a disruption: Parker played Sylvia the dog. "I've never seen a dog portrait in films or on the stage that quite matches the truth and wit of Ms. Parker's performance," wrote a reviewer at *The New York Times*. That could be because she'd performed with Sandy the mutt for twelve straight months in Broadway's *Annie* sixteen years earlier, or it could be because this time, Parker had a mutt of her own to inspire her. Clearly, Parker, who had grown up only with cats, prepared to inhabit the role of Sylvia in

Sarah Jessica Parker played Sylvia the stray.

part by studying Sally, the border collie–Queensland heeler mix she shares with her husband, actor Matthew Broderick. A combination like that makes for a super-intelligent mutt. Not surprisingly, Parker told me, "There are times when I look at Sally and I just know she's *sooo* close to talking!"

Massachusetts artist Carol Lebeaux creates cut-paper silhouettes of dogs as inexpensive family heirlooms.

Town&Country

ESTABLISHED IN 1846

MONGREL MONTHLY

The magazine rack of every muttropolitan home can also reflect mutt pride. Today, there are entire glossy, full-color publications dedicated to dog culture. Some have a particular emphasis on mutts (especially the ones published by animal-welfare organizations). The paws-down best of these, The Bark, has even been called "The New Yorker for dogs," and recently it published a suitably literary compilation of writings about canines. Other picks include Modern Dog, The New York Dog, Fido Friendly, New York Tails, Animal Fair, Best Friends, Animal Guardian, All Animals, Animal Watch, and Protecting Animals. (For subscription information, see appendix, pages 250–251.)

KRANTZ
ON FRED
ASTAIRE

GREAT GUYS:
JIMMY CARTER,
TIGER WOODS,
BEN BRADLEE,
STING AND
MORE

Y 2002
$4.00 CANADA $5.00
REIGN $5.00

05

75470 08833 9

Sally, a border collie–Queensland heeler mix, made the cover of Town & Country in May 2002—as the arm candy of her human, actor Matthew Broderick.

Matthew Broderick with Sally

Do "Shoot" the Dog

No stylish interior is complete without framed family photos. Dedicated mutt people can never have too many dog photographs, but getting a good shot of your one-of-a-kind dog at his or her cutest is no easy task. Our beloved dogs, understandably, can't comprehend why we'd waste time frantically waving our arms trying to get their attention while wielding a contraption that emits a temporarily blinding light. Little wonder professional pet photographers command such steep fees: Getting the "money shot"

is hard work. But with a little patience, practice, and a reliable digital camera (which permits the instant elimination of images that don't do your mutt justice), even nonprofessionals can achieve excellent results. And once they get used to modeling, mutts are natural-born posers who enjoy making love to the camera. Plus, they really know how to tilt their heads just so, drawing attention to their best angle—not to mention their gloriously asymmetrical ears.

Our beloved dogs, understandably, can't comprehend why we'd waste time frantically waving

our arms trying to get their attention while wielding a contraption that emits a temporarily blinding light.

How to get it perfect:

☑ Work outdoors, or in indoor spaces that have ample natural light. Flash can frighten some animals, and it causes the dreaded red-eye effect.

☑ Team up with a friend or family member and have that person stand behind you to make an attention-getting noise with squeaky toys or keys. If your subject is small and camera shy, disguise your photo assistant by draping a large sheet or length of attractive fabric over him or her, and have your assistant cradle the little mutt (so it looks like the dog is cuddled up in fabric).

☑ Use tasty treats as motivation for mutts to assume elegant, photogenic poses.

☑ If eye contact is what you're after, make a high-pitched noise. I like to screech "E" at the uppermost register of my voice; it usually gets everyone's attention.

☑ Remember, black animals disappear against dark backgrounds. For maximum contrast, seek out light-colored backdrops (if you're shooting on the street) or drape white cloth over your mutt's dog bed.

☑ Don't expect your mutt to model patiently for long periods; call a time-out after twenty minutes, and if you're not satisfied with the images you've gotten, take a break and try again later.

Sammy

Travel

Mutts adore traveling with their people, and the feeling is mutual. Hitting the road with dogs gets to the heart of what travel is about: seeing the world with new eyes. And what bespeaks wanderlust more than a mutt with his head out the car window, ears and jowls flapping in the wind?

Because of Trusty's diminutive size, his guardian felt compelled to acquire a car the mini mutt would feel comfortable riding in: the Mini Cooper.

To protect eyes from wind and errant flying particles, there are even canine-specific goggles called Doggles. Because jumping into the car or boat can be tough on older dogs, options for assisting them range from plain metal ramps to the sophisticated, telescoping Twistep, just the thing to assist a dog into a pickup or SUV. Speaking of boats, MaiTai, a chow mix who was adopted from the Boulder Valley Humane Society, is a seaworthy boat hound herself. Her doting people, Anne and Sandy Butterfield, drive her from Colorado to Maine every year for their summer vacation, where the seaworthy mutt enjoys cruising the Penobscot Bay, facing the wind aboard an Oday 40. And yes, of course she wears a flotation vest designed just for canines.

Not that long ago, driving buffs were more concerned about protecting their cars from their dogs. Today, motorists still cover car seats with removable, washable covers (they're widely available at auto stores and at Target and Costco) because pet hairs have a way of taking root and resisting even the industrial-strength

Some mutt fashion statements can be lifesavers, like the flotation vest worn by MaiTai on sailing excursions.

vacuum cleaner at the car wash, and when you decide to sell your wheels, the quality of a car's interior is a strong selling point. But dog people today care just as much, or more, about protecting the dog from the car, doing all they can to prevent potential injury in a crash and making pets as comfortable as possible. And automotive giants are responding to that concern.

In 1999, Saab became the first car company to offer a full line of vehicle accessories designed specifically for dogs, including a restraining system and animal-friendly harness. (Saab consulted with the Humane Society of the United States, which rightly frowns on attaching restraints to collars.) One year later, Ford introduced the similarly equipped "Have Spot, Will Travel" edition of its Focus sedan. For car models that don't have built-in seat belts for dogs, there's the Ruff Rider Roadie Canine Vehicle Restraint Training Harness. And while car seat covers of yore were all about keeping the interior safe from dog emissions, today's car seat covers double as dog travel blankets, complete with cushy fleece backing for shock and liquid absorption. Mutt people also don't leave home without collapsible dog bowls for water and food.

Taking dog safety one step further, General Motors is currently developing sensor technology that will detect infants and pets who have been recklessly left behind in overheating parked cars; upon detection, the vehicle will emit a loud alarm. Never, ever leave any pet in a parked car in warm weather, as temperatures can quickly climb to deadly heights even with the window cracked.

Many dogs get carsick on long trips, but this malady can be prevented with the gentle herbal remedy called Traveler, available from Tasha's Herbs (see appendix, page 251). If your dog has a history of car sickness, sedate her for the journey with diphenhydramine, a.k.a. Benadryl. This is a rare instance when it's okay to administer an over-the-counter human medication to your dog. Give your mutt one milligram of Benadryl per pound of body weight; pills come in 25-milligram doses, so one pill

> "Loews Loves Pets" is the Mantra at that chain's hotels, where the animal room service Menu includes vet-approved Meals.

1301

should be enough for a twenty-five-pound dog, two will suffice for a fifty-pound dog, and so on. Wrap the pill(s) in a small amount of cheese or meat and administer half an hour before the ride. Whether or not they regularly suffer from car sickness, it's best for dogs to travel on empty stomachs.

Mutts Welcome here

Hospitality giants are learning new tricks to get furry guests and their humans to sit and stay. All properties in the Four Seasons chain welcome dogs, as do all of Starwood's W, Sheraton, and Westin properties. "Loews Loves Pets" is the mantra at that chain's hotels, where the animal room service menu includes vet-approved meals "to help pets deal with jet lag and altitude adjustments" (that includes filet mignon for dogs). Rolling out the red carpet for canines is becoming more and more de rigueur. Biscuits on arrival, designer dog beds, and animal-themed DO NOT DISTURB signs were just the beginning. Hotels now offer dog-walking services and wildlife videos for your mutt's viewing pleasure.

Is homesickness an issue? At the Alexis Hotel in Seattle, the concierge will book a session with an animal psychologist. All this has led to a revolution in hotel housekeeping. Cleaning staff at mutt-friendly hotels use vacuums with HEPA filters to remove pet evidence when they sweep the rooms, ensuring the next guest's comfort.

As for going abroad, while many deluxe hotels—and restaurants—in France and Italy welcome dogs of every provenance and size, a number of countries require lengthy, hazardous quarantines (and more than a few enforce breed restrictions, so your pit bull mix won't be welcome in the Netherlands, for instance). But there's hope: The United Kingdom recently relaxed its notorious six-month quarantine, which Elizabeth Taylor and Richard Burton once skirted by taking up residence with their Pekingese on a yacht docked in the Thames.

Doggie baggage

Although pets have been flying in the cargo hold on passenger planes since 1950, they haven't always survived the trip, so the only way to ensure Fido's safe passage is never to let him out of your sight. Worry-free air travel is ensured for mini mutts small enough to fit into airline-approved carriers such as Sherpa bags—soft-sided, under-seat pet carriers, some of which come with wheels and a retractable handle. But the only plane that allowed the jet-setter to book a seat for a large mutt was the Concorde, and that's now grounded. On all major airlines—even United and Midwest, which offer frequent-flyer miles for pets—big dogs must fly in cargo, which is a risky proposition. There have been numerous accounts of mishandled dogs dying in the cargo hold, or carelessly placed on freezing or broiling tarmac to wait for connecting flights. As a result, some airlines no longer allow dogs to fly during summer and winter months.

Other dogs have escaped their travel crates en route. In 2000, New Jersey senator Frank R. Lautenberg shepherded into law the Safe Air Travel Act for Animals, nicknamed the "Boris Bill" for a mutt who, in 1994, escaped his crate while flying on Delta Air Lines from Florida to New York. Boris fled the airport and wandered around Queens for two months before being reunited with his owner, Barbara Listenik. The legislation calls for increasing airlines' liability for damage to pets to $2,500 (previously, shattered guardians were awarded the monetary equivalent of baggage), doubling civil fines that can be imposed by the government to $5,000 per unfortunate pet incident, improving air flow and temperatures in the cargo holds of planes, and establishing a reporting system that would tell people traveling with pets which airlines have the best—and worst—track records in handling companion animals.

Although standards have improved, most big-dog people do what they can to avoid flying with their animals by

Traveling with her dog Karoo, Hilary Swank embodies movie-star glamour, Mutt Maven-style.

Hilary Swank crossed paths with her mutt Karoo while filming *Red Dust* in Graaff-Reinet on the Eastern Cape of South Africa. "I found Karoo while on location," Swank recalls. "I hopped over a fence, and there was this little fat stray looking up at me and thinking, 'Where the heck did she come from?' She was totally flea-ridden, starving, ticks in ears, the whole thing. . . . So I brought her back with me. And now she's in Clint Eastwood movies!" The actress refers to *Million Dollar Baby*, Eastwood's multiple-Oscar-winning underdog story about a woman boxer. In it, Karoo appears with Eastwood's young daughter Morgan (and Swank stars in the title role).

chartering planes and boats, if they can afford it, or traveling long distances by car. For those who do choose to fly, there are variable surcharges for traveling with a dog, which add to the trip's cost, and additional preparations include making sure a mutt has all his inoculations so that he'll be welcome at the destination. Memo to those who refuse to fly: If everyone stays grounded with their dogs, what

incentive will the aviation industry have to improve safety and service? Back in 1950, United Airlines became the first commercial airline to transport family pets, proudly advertising its state-of-the-art travel kennels. I'd like to believe that they want to uphold that proud heritage, and that all airlines want to join in transporting pets safely, to bring that tradition into the twenty-first century.

WHEN FUR FLIES

A new breed of travel agent has emerged to help people who need to move pets out of necessity: companies that specialize in long-distance relocation of people with pets. These include Miami's Lori Travel and Tampa's Air Animal Pet Movers.

transport horses). Dogs with the appropriate health certificates and inoculations can fly in airline-approved crates while their people sit a short flight of stairs away so that they can check up on their best friends during the seven-hour journey.

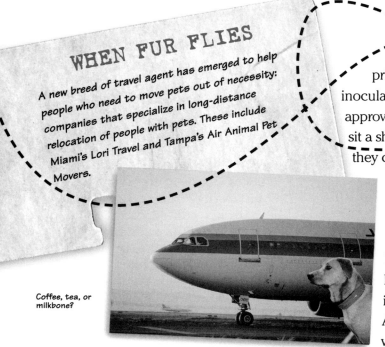

Coffee, tea, or milkbone?

I had a positive experience transporting a rescued Norwegian elkhound from Newark to her new home in Minnesota on Northwest Airlines; my nail-biting tension was greatly calmed when a flight attendant handed me a note prior to takeoff informing me that Elke was safely on board.

With Richard Branson planning to send two-legged tourists to space on Virgin Galactic, it's just a matter of time before some entrepreneur creates an international air carrier just for dog lovers, with passenger seats attached to designer crates. In the meantime, how does one fly a big mutt to Europe? Alitalia will get you there on one of its Boeing 747 cargo planes bound for Milan, equipped with six seats and plenty of storage space (these freighters are regularly used to

When you fly with your dog, do it safely. Just forget about those plastic travel crates; they're easily opened by canine Houdinis, and they won't withstand impact if accidentally dropped, which could result in serious injury. The best containers for travel are made by Tejas Crates. They are practically bullet-proof, made of powder-coated aluminum.

Mutt Mavens worship the dog as it

They're the only crates I'll put my mutts in when I entrust them to the cargo hold. Incidentally, one of the most frequent reasons given for surrendering a mutt to a shelter is moving. But dogs are movable beasts; you *can* take them with you.

As we've seen, some mutts hate feeling cooped up, and they will do their best to escape confinement. That could make airplane travel especially hazardous should your mutt freak out in his crate, escape, and become lost. If your mutt is particularly uncomfortable about being crated, you will have to consider other travel methods. Since tranquilizing dogs prior to air travel is very hazardous and not recommended (it slows their breathing, which puts them at risk of asphyxiation in a pressurized aircraft), you'll have to play it extra safe and travel by car instead. If that's not possible, or you're traveling overseas, leave your mutt at home, in the care of a reputable boarding establishment. Choose one with fun activities, and he may not even notice you were gone!

DOG ALMIGHTY

Many Mutt Mavens worship the dog as if, well, as if dog were god spelled backwards. Stephen Huneck can relate. Renowned for his folk-art-style paintings of dogs, which appear on a range of products from greeting cards to home furnishings, Huneck erected a monument to dog worship: The Dog Chapel. This small, village-style church sits atop Dog Mountain in St. Johnsbury, Vermont. Light streams in through dog-themed stained-glass windows, pews are adorned with dog carvings, and the steeple is topped by a weathervane in the shape of a winged Lab. Instead of holy wafers, there are dog treats. The sign outside reads: "Welcome. All Creeds. All Breeds. No dogmas allowed." The Dog Chapel is open to canines and their human disciples daily, year-round.

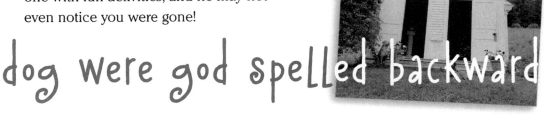

dog were god spelled backwards.

Doggie destinations

With so many wonderful things to do with dogs overseas and at opposite ends of this country, it's a shame to miss them. Here are some of my favorites travel incentives:

Cypress Inn in Carmel-by-the-Sea, California. Part-owned by actress and animal activist Doris Day, there's no leash law on the beach to cramp your mutt's style.

Las Ventanas al Paraíso. At this resort in Los Cabos, Mexico, fitness-conscious Fidos can tag along with you for beach and desert walks and wind down in tandem, too, with a twenty-five-minute side-by-side massage from a therapist trained in human and canine relaxation.

Europeds. This tour company offers Doggie Walk tours of Tuscany, Provence, and the Dordogne, where dogs can accompany their humans to Michelin-starred restaurants and auberges.

FANCY RESTAURANTS IN EUROPEAN CAPITALS

I'll never forget a delicious dinner experience I had at the Vietnamese restaurant Tan Dinh, near the Musée d'Orsay in Paris. The food, decor, and service were exquisite. But best of all, at the table next to mine was a bone-chic trio consisting of an older lady, a younger gentleman, and their enormous *batard,* who assumed his place beneath his humans' table, reclined, and nodded off, as if this were the most natural thing in the world. And you know what? It was.

WORKING LIKE A . . .

Every June, the North Carolina-based Pet Sitters International sponsors "Take Your Dog to Work Day" to encourage petless coworkers to adopt homeless pets from animal shelters. If you've got a dog—and you've secured permission from your employer ahead of time—you can bring your best friend to the office. Of course, many of us who work at home (this writer included) enjoy the presence of a coworker mutt, or several, every day of the year. A mutt named Radar, a.k.a. the weather dog, is the telegenic mascot of the meteorologists at Channel 2 in Houston, Texas; he was adopted from the Houston Humane Society. And many offices also have quadruped mascots on the premises year-round, including the ultimate pet-friendly workplace: Replacements, Ltd. of Greensboro, North Carolina, which boasts the world's largest selection of old and new china and crystal. Employees are encouraged to bring dogs to work with them, so as many as seventy-five dogs punch in on an average day. According to Replacements' owner-founder Bob Page, "Not a single piece of our inventory has ever been damaged by a pet." Smart businesses would do well to follow Replacements' lead. According to a study by the Connecticut-based American Pet Products Manufacturing Association, absenteeism dropped 27 percent, and 58 percent of employees stayed at the office later, if there was a pet on the premises. The study also showed that pets lowered stress levels and raised productivity at 73 percent of companies polled—plus fewer smokers were found at pet-friendly offices. This may explain why more and more companies are allowing employees to bring pets to the office more than just once a year.

his pal Friday

The study showed that pets lowered stress levels and raised productivity at 73 percent of companies polled.

DOG BLOG

Picture a cyber dog park,

where mutts from all over the country have their own Web page complete with photos, touching tributes, bios detailing their nicknames (most have at least one), favorite foods, pet peeves, and inspirational tales of adoption and rescue. That's Dogster.com. The popular site went live in January 2004 with just one hundred dogs; it's multiplied exponentially. For Web surfers who have dogs, Dogster.com is a way to sing the praises of puppy love by posting photos of beloved pets online. For the dogless, it's an immersion course in canine culture and an excellent outlet for mutt appreciation. Dogster's tag line is "For the Love of Dog," and it shows.

For Web surfers who have dogs

Love Mutts

Afton + Brendan xxx

Some mutts have a nose for romance, so if you're single, a mixed breed can be your best escort.

Some women take gay male friends to parties as "walkers"; others simply walk their dogs. Need compelling incentive for including your mutt in your extracurricular activities? Consider this: In 1993, a collie mix named Wile E. accompanied her human, actress Afton Smith, to Winona Ryder's Fourth of July barbecue. During the party, Wile E. wandered off and encountered the actor Brendan Fraser; when Smith went looking for her dog, she met her match. The couple were married not long after that. For non-Hollywood types, several online dating services connect animal lovers with other animal lovers. (See appendix, page 252 for more details.)

Brendan and Afton Fraser with their mutt match-maker, Wile E. (center) in a portrait by Christopher Ameruoso.

Flossie and Drew Barrymore work their persuasive powers on Demi Moore.

Estella Warren appeared with her mutt in this advertisement for Cartier's "Kiss of the Dragon" collection.

TOOTH IN ADVERTISING

Mutts can be very persuasive, especially when they're sharing the limelight with beautiful people, as Isaac Mizrahi's dog Harry did in a recent advertisement for Target. Actress Estella Warren appeared in an ad for the renowned jeweler Cartier alongside her beloved mutt Smasher. "He's the best dog in the entire world, super sweet, with more personality than any dog I've ever had, plus he's an amazing jumper," Warren says. Mutts have helped to brand other luxury goods as well. Oenophiles appreciate how a surprising mix of ingredients can create something memorable with a complex bouquet to be prized and savored. But few appreciate this phenomenon more than Brenda and Chris Lynch, proprietors of Sonoma County's Mutt Lynch Winery, named for the couple's two mixed breeds, Max and Nicki. Among the winery's unique offerings are "Merlot Over and Play Dead," "Unleashed Chardonnay," and "Canis Major Zinfandel," each bottle's label sporting a painted canine portrait.

And yet, mutts are perhaps most persuasive when exerting their influence behind the scenes. Rumor has it that Demi Moore was reluctant to take a role in actress-producer Drew Barrymore's pet project *Charlie's Angels*--until, that is, Barrymore and her posse of Hollywood-player mutts deployed their persuasive charms. Flossie, a onetime stray, is top dog chez Barrymore, because she alerted Drew to the fire that burned down their home. To show her gratitude, Barrymore willed her new house to Flossie.

"He's the best dog in the entire world..."

MUTT MILITANTS, UNITE!

Don't make the mistake of maligning mutts, because mutt people will notice, and their response will be swift and fierce. In 2003, the Boar's Head brand of luncheon meat, in an effort to drum up publicity for its frankfurters, unveiled an advertisement featuring a gleaming, barbecued hot dog with the tagline "Makes Other Dogs Taste Like Mutts." The company was deluged with letters, and the ads discreetly disappeared.

Member of the Wedding

Adding any new family member--regardless of species—changes the family dynamic. Sometimes the changes are minor; other times they'll require creative thinking to smooth over.

Let's say you're introducing a new love interest to your mutt. Before you have this new person over, move the dog's bed outside of your bedroom (if that's where your mutt currently resides) and make him sleep there several days a week. This might be painful at first, but you'll thank yourself later. If the new person in your life becomes a frequent overnight guest, you can slowly reintroduce the dog into the bedroom. Just be sure the dog does not sleep between you and your partner. He should be off to one side or at the foot of the bed, lest he start to think he's in control of your relationship.

If the love connection leads to marriage, consider inviting your mutt to your wedding. Including the dog adds a poignant, personal touch to important occasions, and more and more animal lovers are including mutts in weddings, whether as guests or as ring-bearers (in the latter case, the dog carries the ring in a pouch affixed to his collar or harness).

When Elana Frankel married Dan Tashman at New York's Guastavino's restaurant in May 2004, the couple's friends and family were hardly surprised

> If the love connection leads to marriage, consider inviting your mutt to your wedding.

Cassidy stood up-- actually, she lay down--for her best man, Dan Tashman, at his wedding to Elana Frankel.

to see another female walking down the aisle with the groom: a mutt named Cassidy. "Cassidy is a member of our immediate family, so we couldn't imagine having a wedding without her," Frankel explains. When incorporating four-legged friends in weddings, preparing the dog for the big day is high on the list of prenuptial priorities.

Dogs at weddings must do more than look their best; they must behave impeccably. Although Cassidy is quite mellow, Frankel and Tashman did the right thing by boning up on training basics. Whoever will be walking Fido down the aisle should take him to as many different public places as possible

beforehand. Have the dog sit and stay, giving him a reward when he complies, so he learns to stay relaxed while surrounded by people and activity. Also practice the down-stay command, especially if the ceremony is long and your dog is older. If your dog will be wearing a flower or bow tie, put the ornament on for a few minutes every day, then reward with a treat. Repeat the process until the dog is totally oblivious to the ornament.

Don't forget to brief your wedding photographer on a list of desired dog shots so you'll always have proof of how your mutt attendant rose to the occasion.

Political Correctness and the Mutt

Nowadays we say executive assistant or flight attendant or cleaning person. Prisons are correctional facilities; welfare is public assistance. Well, animal-adoption lingo has also kept pace with the times. Just as owners are now guardians, pets are companion animals, dog runs are off-leash areas, pounds are animal shelters, and mutts are classified as mixes.

Come on, my fellow Mutt Mavens: Let's take back and embrace the M-word with love.

Following is a comprehensive listing of resources, services, and shelters discussed in the foregoing chapters. To contact the author, e-mail js@pet-reporter.com.

Intro & Chapter 1

Perfectly in tune with contemporary pop culture's embrace of the mixed-breed dog are animal-welfare groups that proudly incorporate the words *mutt* or *stray* in their names:

Stray Pride: 800-200-7338, www.socialteez.com

Stray From the Heart: 212-726-DOGS, www.strayfromtheheart.org

Mighty Mutts: mightymutts@hotmail.com, http://mightymutts.tripod.com

To learn more about the Puerto Rican *sato,* and to inquire about adopting one, visit www.saveasato.org.

Humane Society of Grand Bahama: www.gbhumane.org

Rep. Marsha Blackburn of Tennessee adopted Indy and Betty from Williamson County Animal Control, 615-790-5590, www.williamsoncounty-tn.org.

To reach **Martha Barnette,** visit www.funwords.com; her local animal shelter is the Kentucky Humane Society, www.kyhumane.org.

Arnell Memorial Humane Society, Amery, WI: 715-268-7387

Great American Mutt Contest, sponsored by Tails in Need: 212-327-3160, www.greatamericanmuttshow.com

Chapter 2

American Kennel Club (AKC): 212-696-8200, www.akc.org

Westminster Kennel Club: 212-213-3165, www.westminsterkennelclub.org

Peace Plantation: 607-865-5759, www.ppasny.org

Shelters across the country are overflowing with pit bulls and pit mixes; there are also rescue organizations that specialize in this lovable, misunderstood nonbreed, including:

Bay Area Doglovers Responsible About Pitbulls (BADRAP): www.badrap.org

Casa del Toro: www.casadeltoro.org

Second Chance Animal Rescue & Adoptions: www.secondchancedogs.org

Monmouth County SPCA: 732-542-2030, www.monmouthcountyspca.org

Bless the Bullys: www.blessthebullys.com

Last Chance Pits: http://last-chance-pits.tripod.com

Out of the Pits: www.outofthepits.org

For more, contact **Pit Bull Rescue Central:** www.pbrc.net.

For information on **Scruffts,** visit www.scruffts.co.uk.

To learn more about the horrors of puppy mills, visit **www.awarenessday.org.**

The shelter that took in pups Trigger, Remington, Winchester, and Colt is **Escambia County Animal Control,** Pensacola, FL, 850-595-3075.

For information on **Lynda Barry,** visit www.marlysmagazine.com.

Adopting a mutt is as easy as visiting your local animal shelter. For information on **National Animal Shelter Appreciation Week,** in November, visit www.hsus2.org/sheltering/general/nasaw-intro.html. For those who'd like to combine the process with a fun road trip, if time and funds allow, make the trip to the shelter an event by driving to an animal sanctuary. As an alternative to visiting a densely populated urban animal shelter, you can visit animals (including farm animals like horses and pigs) in a wider, more open, rural space. Sanctuary visits make for great family trips— the kids will love it—and if you're approved for adoption, you can drive away with a new family member: one of the sanctuary's resident mutts.

Best Friends (www.bestfriends.org) is a gorgeous destination in the red-rock country of Southern Utah, with the white cliffs of Zion National Park looming in the distance. The sanctuary offers lodging in the Angel Canyon Guest Cottages on the sanctuary grounds, overlooking the horse pastures.

Hearts United for Animals (www.hua.org) operates two sanctuaries in Nebraska, one on forty acres, where mutts romp in fenced fields, and a new sixty-five-acre compound with a visitors' park and picnic tables.

Explore the picturesque Catskill Mountain region of upstate New York with a visit to one of these shelters:

Animal Haven Acres, in South Kortight: 607-538-9117, www.animalhavenshelter.org

Pets Alive, in Middletown: 845-386-9738, www.petsalive.com

Peace Plantation in Walton: 607-865-5759, www.ppasny.org

AKC Companion Animal Recovery: www.akccar.org. To report a lost pet, call their 24-hour hotline, 800-252-7894; have the pet's collar tag, microchip, or tattoo ID number ready and press 1 to speak to a recovery coordinator. This database has information on animals injected with the **Home Again chip** (www.homeagainid.com). Another form of permanent identification is the **Avid Microchip** (www.avidmicrochip.com).

ASPCA: 212-876-7700, www.aspca.org

Bide-A-Wee: 212-532-6395, www.bideawee.org

ARF (Animal Rescue Fund of the Hamptons): 631-537-0400, www.arfhamptons.org

Petfinder: www.petfinder.com

PETsMART: 623-580-6100, www.petsmart.com

Petco: 877-738-6742, www.petco.com

Biscuits & Bath Doggy Village (212-692-2323, www.biscuitsandbath.com) features adoptables from **Animal Haven Shelter** (718-886-3683, www.animalhavenshelter.org).

Strut Your Mutt: 801-364-0379, www.utahpets.org

Nob Hill Pooch Parade (Animal Humane Association of New Mexico): 505-255-5523, www.ahanm.org

Doggie Dash: 503-285-7722, www.oregonhumane.org

Alabama's **Montgomery Humane Society** has an annual pet photo contest to raise funds for shelter animals: 334-409-0622, www.montgomeryhumane.com.

Brooklyn Animal Resource Coalition: 718-486-7489, www.barcshelter.org

Blue Dog Rescue: www.bluedogrescue.com

DogFest: www.dogfestfilmfestival.org

Lint Roller Party and Save a Stray Soiree: 801-364-0379, www.utahpets.org

Fur Ball: 919-772-2326, www.spcawake.org

San Diego Humane Society: www.sdhumane.org

DogHaus: www.spcadoghaus.org

New York City Animal Care & Control: 212-788-4000, www.nycacc.org

Critter Knitters Coalition: www.critterknitters.org

The Snuggles Project: www.h4ha.org/snuggles/

Knit & Purl for Pets, St. Louis, MO: 636-537-2322, ext. 28

To subscribe to **EVerseRadio,** a weekly column of literary, publishing, and arts information and opinion (it's free), e-mail everseradio@earthlink.net.

Humane Society of New York: 212-752-4840, www.humanesocietyny.org

Below is a partial nationwide listing of 24-hour emergency vet hospitals:

California

VCA Emergency Animal Hospital
and Referral Center
San Diego, CA
619-299-2400
www.vcai.com

VCA-West Los Angeles Animal Hospital
Los Angeles, CA
310-473-2951
www.westernu.edu/xp/edu/veterinary/vcahospital.xml

California Veterinary Specialists
Murrieta, CA
951-600-9803
www.californiavetspecialists.com

Mutts cartoonist Patrick McDonnell illustrates the draw of the animal shelter: unconditional love.

Colorado
Alameda East Animal Medical Center
Denver, CO
303-366-2639
www.alamedaeast.com

Florida
Animal Emergency Clinic
St. Petersburg, FL
727-323-1311
(after hours only; not open during the day)

Georgia
Cobb Veterinary Emergency &
  Referral Center
Marietta, GA
770-424-9157
www.cobbevc.com

Illinois
Dundee Animal Hospital
Dundee, IL
847-428-6114

Massachusetts
Foster Hospital for Small Animals
Tufts University
North Grafton, MA
508-839-5395

New York
Bobst Hospital, Animal Medical Center
New York City, NY
212-838-8100
www.amcny.org

Center for Specialized Veterinary Care
Westbury, NY
516-420-0000
www.vetspecialist.com

Cornell University Hospital
  for Animals
Ithaca, NY
607-253-3060
www.vet.cornell.edu/hospital

Ohio
Animal Emergency & Medical Hospital
Columbus, OH
614-889-2556

MedVet
Columbus, OH
614-846-5800, www.medvet-cves.com

Oregon
Dove Lewis Emergency Animal Hospital
Portland, OR
503-228-7281
www.dovelewis.org

Pennsylvania
Matthew J. Ryan Veterinary Hospital
University of Pennsylvania
215-898-4685
www.vet.upenn.edu/ryan

Texas
For a hospital in your area, contact
the Veterinary Emergency and Critical
Care Society, San Antonio, TX
210-698-5575
www.veccs.org.

Fort Worth Animal Medical Center
Fort Worth, TX
817-560-8387
www.fortworth.nationalpet.com

Gulf Coast Veterinary Specialists
Houston, TX
713-693-1100
www.gcvs.com

Texas A&M Veterinary Hospital
College Station, TX
979-845-2351
www.cvm.tamu.edu/vsam/

Washington
Veterinary Specialty Center of Seattle
Lynnwood, WA
425-697-6106
www.seattleveterinaryspecialists.com

No dog is more grateful than a shelter mutt.

Veterinary Teaching Hospital
Washington State University
Pullman, WA
509-335-0711
www.vetmed.wsu.edu/depts-vth

Wisconsin
Animal Emergency Center
Milwaukee, WI
414-540-6710
www.animalemergencycenter.com

Mayor's Alliance for NYC's Animals:
www.animalalliancenyc.org

To learn about purebred dogs' physical characteristics, which will help you recognize distinctive mutt features, consult the AKC's *Complete Dog Book*, www.akc.org.

Kirby of postage-stamp fame isn't the first mutt mascot of the U.S. Postal Service. **Owney, a.k.a. "Globe-trotter,"** was a mutt found abandoned outside an Albany post office in 1888. Postal workers brought the shivering stray inside and covered him in mail bags to keep him warm. Owney never forgot the kindness, and felt most secure and comfortable when surrounded by mail bags. He spent the next ten years following mail bags wherever they went, traveling by rail and logging over 140,000 miles. Owney died in 1897, and his body was stuffed and mounted. Today, wearing the vest he wore in life, decorated with tags from all over the country and the world, Owney is on permanent display at the Smithsonian's National Postal Museum in Washington, D.C. (www.postalmuseaum. si.edu).

Wolfsong Ranch Foundation:
505-557-2354, www.wolfsongranch.org

A few breed-specific rescue groups that are overwhelmed and could use some help:

Dalmatian Rescue:
www.dalmatianrescue.com

Koss Dalmatian Rescue:
718-522-4782 or 860-626-0017

Boston Terrier Rescue: www.btrescue.org, www.bostonrescue.net

Great Dane Rescue: Mid-Atlantic Great Dane Rescue League (MAGDRL), www.magdrl.org

Jack Russell Rescue:
www.recycledrussells.com

German Shorthaired Pointer Rescue:
www.gsprescue.org

Beagles and More:
770-442-1956

Great Pyrenees Rescue of Greater Chicago: 847-668-7297,
www.gpcgc.org/rescue.htm

Chapter 3

The upstate New York animal shelter where I adopted Tiki and Sheba is the **Delaware Valley Humane Society,**
607-563-7780.

To learn more about AKC-recognized breeds as well as those that are not recognized by the AKC, including the Leonberger and Berger de Picard, consult *DK Handbooks: Dogs* by David Alderton (Dorling Kindersley Publishing), available on Amazon.com.

Dog treat vending machine (dispenses Liver Biscotti) by **Street Treats:** www.streettreats.com

Melissa Holbrook Pierson adopted Nelly from **West Virginia's Animal Friends of Barbour County:** www.afobcwv.org.

Special thanks to the animal shelters and rescue organizations that brought dogs to our Mutt Family Tree photo shoot:

Animal Haven:
718-886-3683, www.animalhavenshelter.org

Humane Society of New York:
212-752-4840,
www.humanesocietyny.org

Bide-A-Wee: 212-532-6395, www.bideawee.org

Miss Rumples' Orphanage
(specializes in small-dog adoption):
missrumplesorphanage@verizon.net,
www.missrumplesorphanage.com

Koss Dalmatian Rescue:
718-522-4782

Animal Care & Control of New York City:
212-788-4000, www.nycacc.org

Northstar Placement: 845-623-2362,
www.northstarplacement.petfinder.com

If you see a mutt you like in this chapter, give one of these shelters a call. "Adopt Me" indicates that a dog was still available at press time.

Chapter 4

Jeff Hephner adopted Betty from **North Shore Animal League,**
516-883-7575, www.nsalamerica.org.

To locate a veterinary homeopath near you, contact the **Academy of Veterinary Homeopathy,** 866-652-1590, www.theavh.org.

To locate a veterinarian practicing complementary and alternative medicine, go to **www.altvetmed.org.**

Russell and Kimora Lee Simmons agree that black mutts are beautiful. "All my animals are black," she says.

For veterinarian referrals, contact the **American Veterinary Medical Assocation** (AVMA), 847-925-8070, www.avma.org.

To locate an animal hospital near you, contact the **American Animal Hospital Association** (AAHA), 303-986-2800, www.aahanet.org.

For a **specialist,** call or write the American College of Veterinary Internal Medicine (ACVIM), 800-245-9081, www.acvim.org.

Diatomaceous earth is available from Perma-Guard, 615-370-4301, www.biconet.com.

For those who still wish to pursue pet insurance despite my caveats:

www.petcareinsurance.com

www.vetinsurance.com

www.petplan.com

www.petshealthplan.com

www.petassure.com

Some mutts *really* hate feeling confined. If your mutt has an injury that requires him to wear an E-collar (a conelike contraption that prevents dogs from bothering wounds so they may heal undisturbed), he could revolt against it and begin bucking around like a bronco; this happened to my Tiki. The comfortable alternative is the **Bite Not Collar** (www.bitenot.com), which limits a dog's ability to reach a wound without obstructing his vision or impeding his ability to sleep and play. Available from JB Wholesale Pet Supplies, 800-526-0388, www.jbpet.com.

Premium pet foods:

Natural Balance: 800-829-4493, www.naturalbalanceinc.com

Merrick: 800-664-7387, www.merrickpetcare.com

Nature's Variety Prairie: available at The Pet Stop, NYC, www.petstopnyc.com

Solid Gold: 800-364-4863, www.solidgoldhealth.com

Innova, California Natural, and Karma: 800-532-7261, www.naturapet.com

Azmira: 800-497-5665, www.azmira.com

Wysong: 800-748-0188, www.wysong.net

Eagle Pack Holistic Select: 800-255-5959, www.eaglepack.com

Active Life: 877-291-2913, www.activelifepp.com

Newman's Own:
www.newmansownorganics.com

Pet Guard: www.petguard.com

Lick Your Chops: www.integratedpet.com

Flint River Ranch: 866-236-5102,
www.flintriver.com

Pinnacle: available at
www.redbandannapetfood.com

O & M: 888-881-7703,
www.ompetproducts.com

Strive: www.strivepetfoods.com

Artemis: www.artemiscompany.com

Timber Wolf Organics: 863-439-0049,
www.timberwolforganics.com

Canidae: www.canidae.com

For dogs displaying symptoms of food allergies,
Purina HA is a hypoallergenic formula,
developed by a veterinarian and a molecular
biologist, that's available by a vet's prescription.
For information, ask your vet or visit
www.purina.com.

As important as what a mutt eats is the
bowl he eats from; avoid plastic bowls unless
they are made of human-food-grade plastic
(such as the bowls made by Cats Rule/Dogs 2,
www.catsrule.com). **Alessi** (www.alessi.com),
the firm headquartered in Omegna, Italy, and
renowned since 1921 for high-design kitchen
utensils and tableware, recently introduced
the stunning "Lupita" dog bowl—a portion of
proceeds from sales of the Lupita are donated
to the Omegna Municipal Dog Kennel to help
out *razzi misti Italiani* (a.k.a. *bastardini,* or Italian
mutts)—available at Karikter, 415-434-1120,
212-274-1966, www.karikter.com.

**People for the Ethical Treatment of
Animals:** 757-622-PETA, www.peta.org

Dr. Harvey's Canine Health: available from
www.naturespet.com

The mutt is
everybody's
all-American,
so why not
serve him
meals in the
All-American Dog
bowl by Harry Barker?
www.harrybarker.com

For stores that carry **Orange Guard Spray:**
www.orangeguard.com

Another natural, citrusy insecticide that's
safe to use around pets is **Bugs-R-Done,**
www.bugsrdone.com.

The best grooming products:

Mellow Mutts: 800-830-1762,
www.mellowmutts.com

Fauna: 800-536-1909,
www.faunapet.com

SheaPet: 888-SHEAPET, www.sheapet.com

Aesop: www.aesop.net.au

Julien Farel Salon: 212-888-8988,
www.julienfarel.com

Nail clipper from **The Pet Stop:** 212-580-2400, www.petstopnyc.com

Toothbrush from **Vet Solutions:** 817-529-7500, www.vetsolutions.com

Na-mutt-ste! Crunch, the national fitness chain, offers a summer course in "Ruff Yoga" for people and dogs; www.crunch.com.

Here are some books on yoga and dogs and how you can unwind with your mutt:

Home Alone: Tools to Help Pets Overcome Separation by Bruce Eric Van Horn

Doga: Yoga for Dogs by Jennifer Brilliant and William Berloni

Bow Wow Yoga: 10,000 Years of Posturing by Gerry Olin

To order *Wait for the Sunset* and other harp music CDs by **Susan Raimond,** call 800-971-1044 or e-mail petpause2000@yahoo.com.

Secure your garbage in a quality trash bin so your scavenging mutt has fewer opportunities to plunder it (and always toss out the trash when leaving a mutt home alone):

Polder bullet trash bin: available at www.kitchensource.com

Brabantia Touch Bin: available at www.everythinghome.com

To maximize your mutt's nighttime visibility, a range of illuminated dog collars are available from **See Fido,** 800-305-7404, www.seefido.com.

Some ritzy dog day care facilities:

L.A. Dogworks: 323-461-5151, www.ladogworks.com

The Loved Dog, L.A.: 310-914-3033, www.theloveddog.com

Bow Wow Lounge, Chicago: 773-525-0277, www.bowwowlounge.com

Biscuits & Bath Doggy Village, New York: 212-692-2323, www.biscuitsandbath.com

WoofSpa, New York: 212-229-9663, www.woofspaandresort.com

New York Dog Spa & Hotel: 212-206-7980, www.dogspa.com

Brooklyn Dog House, New York: 718-222-4900, www.brooklyndoghouse.com

The Common Dog, Boston: 617-381-6363, www.commondog.com

Urban Fauna, Portland, OR: 503-223-4602, www.urbanfauna.com

To learn about gem therapy, contact **Gemisphere:** 800-727-8877, www.gemisphere.com.

To learn about **organic flower essences,** e-mail green.hope.farm@valley.net or visit www.greenhopeessences.com (be sure to order a free catalog).

Dr. Ada González of Gemisphere demonstrates the healing power of gemstones on Lexus, a mutt up for adoption at Animal Haven. Check out those necklaces!

To reach **Vicki Draper,** who practices craniosacral therapy and jin shin acupressure, visit www.vickidraper.com.

Deoderize pet stains with Odor Eliminator, www.sea-yu.com.

Environmentally friendly cleaners (they also make laundry detergents):

Ecover: www.ecover.com

Seventh Generation:
800-456-1191, www.seventhgen.com

Method: 866-963-8463, www.methodhome.com

Sun & Earth: 800-298-7861, www.sunandearth.com

LifeTree: 800-347-5211, www.goturtle.com

Now Foods Pure Lavender Oil: available at www.nowfoods.com

Selma Blair adopted Wink from **The Lange Foundation,** 310-473-5585, www.langefoundation.com.

Grieving for a mutt is indescribably difficult. Here are a few resources to help ease the transition with counseling:

Animal Medical Center: 212-838-8100, www.amcny.org

Dove Lewis: 503-228-7281, www.dovelewis.org

Center for Specialized Veterinary Care:
516-420-0000, www.vetspecialist.com

Association for Pet Loss and Bereavement:
718-382-0690, www.aplb.org

Some people are, understandably, concerned that the ashes returned to them are not those of their beloved dog. If you wish to watch as your mutt's body is placed in the crematory and wait until the process is complete, consult **Dignified Pet Services** in Portland, OR: 503-885-2211, www.dignifiedpetservices.com.

Many call themselves animal communicators; these three are the real thing: **Kay Mann,** 607-785-3852; **Cindy Smith,** 828-686-4564, www..animalsmith.com; **Rose DeDan,** 206-933-7877, www.reikishamanic.com.

To highlight the bond between canine and human seniors, the National Council of Jewish Women in New York City holds an annual senior-pet adoptathon. For information, call 212-687-5030 or visit www.ncjw.org.

Chapter 5

To locate a professional dog trainer in your area, contact the **Association of Pet Dog Trainers:** 800-PET-DOGS, www.apdt.com.

For information on **Sinbad the mutt,** visit www.pawpatrol24-7.net or www.csfa.net/storefront/workinlikeadog.asp

The best nonfancy crates on the market are made by **Midwest:** 800-428-8560, www.midwesthomes4pets.com. Be advised that despite the name, these are not permanent "homes" for pets—just temporary devices to aid in training so that your mutt may share your home and respect it and your belongings.

For the designer take on the crate, there's **BowHaus:** 888-588-2295, www.bowhaus.ca.

Wee-Wee Pads are available at pet-supply stores everywhere; for a store near you, call 631-434-1100 or visit www.fourpaws.com.

For information on **Maddie's Pet Adoption Center,** call 415-522-3500 or visit www.sfspca.org.

The puppies on pages 150–151 are from a litter of rottweiler-shepherd mixes rescued by the **ASPCA,** America's first humane organization (www.aspca.org).

Lupine collars: 800-228-9653, www.lupinepet.com

Gentle Leader: 888-640-8840, www.gentleleader.com

Softouch SENSE-ation Harness: 866-305-6145, www.softouchconcepts.com

Solid Gold Tiny Tots Jerky Treats: 800-364-4863, www.solidgoldhealth.com

Real Meat Treats: 800-454-PETS, www.realmeattreats.com

Dogswell treats: 888-559-8833, www.dogswell.com

A canine ponders the big issues in a *Mutts* strip by Patrick McDonnell.

Dog Trainer Sue Nastasi of Dogs-in-the-Hood Training (www.dogsinthehood.com/training.htm) works with her mutt Billie on the "Sit Pretty" trick.

Poe was adopted from the **Animal Shelter of The Wood River Valley,** Hailey, ID, 208-788-4351, www.animalshelterwrv.org.

If you absolutely must use a muzzle in a pinch, the one that will least victimize your mutt is the No Bark/No Bite Comfort Muzzle, available at **Pet Edge,** 800-738-3343, www.petedge.com.

United States Dog Agility Association: 972-487-2200, www.usdaa.com

North American Dog Agility Council: www.nadac.com

"We're the mutts with the Constitution!"

—Bill Murray in the movie *Stripes*

Combining agility and Broadway-style showmanship, Tom and Bonnie Brackney travel to perform with their troupe of rescued mixed breeds, **The Madcap Mutts:** www.madcapmutts.com.

Because the famous Benji is a shelter mutt, director-producer Joe Camp's mission is "to change the face of adoption by branding all adoptable shelter pets as **'Benji's Buddies'**"; to learn more, visit www.benjisbuddies.com.

Ally Sheedy's pet charity is A Cause for Paws, www.acauseforpaws.com.

If you and your mutt are interested in volunteering in your community as pet-therapy partners, contact one of the following organizations:

Delta Society: 425-226-7357, www.deltasociety.org

Therapy Dogs International: 973-252-9800, www.tdi-dog.org

Bide-A-Wee: 212-532-6395, www.bideawee.org

Good Dog Foundation: 888-859-9992, www.thegooddogfoundation.org

People and Animals Who Serve (PAAWS): 541-461-1188, www.peopleandanimalswhoserve.org

While working at Ground Zero, Hoss wore **protective boots** from www.dogbooties.com, 218-727-3121. The animal shelter that took Hoss in twice is the **Bonnie L. Hays Small Animal Shelter,** Hillsboro, OR, 503-846-7041.

The dogs pictured on page 178 are **hearing dog Kira**, a black basenji mix adopted from an animal shelter and traind by Paws With a Cause, and **Oliver,** a retriever mix with Fidos for Freedom, who works as a mobility-assistance dog.

For organizations that certify mixed breeds service dogs, assisting the physically challenged, contact:

Assistance Dogs International: www.adionline.org

Great Plains Assistance Dogs: 701-685-2242, www.alert-dog.com

Fidos for Freedom: 301-490-4005, www.fidosforfreedom.org

William Berloni Theatrical Animals: www.theatricalanimals.com

To contact **Rikke Brogaard,** visit www.rikkebdogtraining.com.

For a **Clicker Training starter kit:** 800-47-CLICK, www.clickertraining.com

Chapter 6

Beds for dogs:

Garden Retreat wrought-iron bed by Lulu Jane: available at www.pamperedpuppy.com or www.lulujane.com

Eloise Inc.: 866-ELOISES, www.eloiseinc.com

Bark Deco: 310-948-5522, www.barkdeco.com

Travel Bed by Canine Hardware: 800-660-9033, www.caninehardware.com

A Queen Anne–style settee upholstered in "Hound in the Round" fabric by William Wegman for Crypton. Upholstery by J&P Decorators, 718-482-8500.

Quilted moving blankets: available from Movers Supply House, 800-4321-MSH

Plastic bread trays: available from T.M. Fitzgerald, 888-795-0660, www.tmfitzgerald.com

Kuranda dog beds: www.kuranda.com

Donut Bed by **Bowsers**: available at www.perfectdogbeds.com

To help keep dog bedding smelling fresh, spritz with **Mellow Mutts Bed Boost:** 800-830-1762, www.mellowmutts.com.

Lucite cube available from **Plexi-Craft:** 800-24-PLEXI, www.plexi-craft.com

Bettie dog toy available at **Postmodern Pets:** 650-331-3500, www.postmodernpets.com

Bodhi toys available from **Nature's Pet:** 201-796-0627, www.naturespet.com

Planet Dog Orbee: available at www.muttropolis.com

LA Eyeworks: www.laeyeworks.com; eyeglasses chew toy available at Myoptics, 212-334-3123, www.myoptics.com

No mutt can resist the primordial chew toy: a raw beef bone. K. E. Rush & Sons offers organic raw bones for dogs; to order, call 215-412-4110 or visit www.natures-intent.com.

For stores that carry **Kong:** 303-216-2626, www.kongcompany.com

ChuckIt! Ball Launcher (helps you throw a mean tennis ball) and **Flying Squirrel** (safer for dogs' teeth than a conventional flying disc) by Canine Hardware: www.caninehardware.com, available at www.barkerandmeowsky.com, 773-868-0200.

Animal Planet Toss a Turtle is a flying disc made of rubber that floats; for stores, contact **Premier Pet Products,** 800-933-5595 or www.premier.com.

For stores carrying **BOODA** rope bones: 800-289-4738, www.aspenpet.com

Breath-A-Licious dental bone: available at 888-644-7297, www.dancingpaws.com

TireBiter toys available from Mammoth Pet: 888-738-2008, www.mammothpet.com

Cheeky Squeaky Pets by Wendy Ann Gardner for Nylabone: 800-631-2188, www.nylabone.com

Snooks Sweet Potato Dog Chews: to order, e-mail gotsnook7@earthlink.net.

A substitute for pig's ears is the lookalike (and soundalike) **Piggears,** www.cardinalpet.com.

Burberry: www.burberry.com

Dog booties: 218-727-3121, www.dogbooties.com

Musher's Secret: available at HandsNPaws, 973-594-9889, www.handsnpaws.com

For stores carrying **Safe Paw Ice Melter:** 800-783-7841, www.safepaw.com

For those interested in making their own mutt sweaters, a New York City yarn shop called **Gotta Knit!** offers a beginners' course in knitting for dog lovers: 212-989-3030 or www.gottaknit.net.

"Soft collar," a combination collar-harness made of light mesh in bright colors by Puppia World, available at **Posh Paws:** 212-410-5360 or www.poshpawstallandsmall.com

A velvet jingle-bell collar is a low-stress way to dress a mutt for the holidays. It's available from **Canine Styles:** 212-838-2064, www.caninestyles.com.

Holiday antlers (on Pepper) from **Orvis:** www.orvis.com

Ultrasuede: 917-342-8486, www.ultrasuede.com

Chella: 805-560-8400, www.chellatextiles.com

Lee Jofa: 800-453-3563, www.leejofa.com

Crypton Super Fabrics are extraordinary: water, drool, and other liquids roll right off them. In addition to by-the-yard upholstery material, Crypton offers premade pet beds as well as a design-your-own pet bed program, where customers may choose from a range of canine-themed patterns designed by William Wegman (for photo, see page 248) plus coordinating solids: call 800-CRYPTON or visit www.cryptonfabric.com.

SureFit Slipcovers: 800-305-5857, www.surefit.net

J&P Decorators is the clear-vinyl-slipcover specialist: 718-482-8500.

Scamp Ramp: e-mail scamps@cox.net, www.scampsonline.com

Lonseal: 310-830-7111, www.lonseal.com

"Adopt Me" wallpaper by **Tyler Hall:** 212-239-0362, www.tyler-hall.com

Interface FLOR: 866-281-3567, www.interfaceflor.com

Petal Cleanse available at WBUY: 800-643-WBUY, www.allergic2pets.com

Dyson DC14 Animal: available at Target stores (www.target.com) or visit www.dyson.com

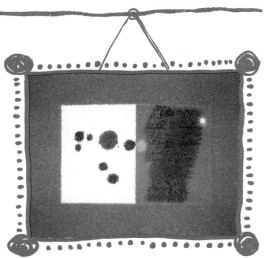

Tibino and Sheba Have a Night Out celebrates the attraction between artist Bettina Werner's dalmatian (Tibino) and my mutt Sheba.

Redi-Shades: available at 888-608-6611, www.redi-shade.com

For stores that carry **Benjamin Moore paint,** visit www.benjaminmoore.com.

Doyle New York: 212-427-2730, www.doylenewyork.com

Martha Szabo has been called "The Alice Neel of Pets": www.marthaszabo.com.

Elizabeth Peyton: c/o Gavin Brown's Enterprise, 212-627-5258, www.gavinbrown.biz

Kenny Scharf: e-mail info@kennyscharf.com, www.kennyscharf.com

Roy Kortick: 718-387-7887

Jennifer Weinik: 215-740-7471, www.jweinik.com

Patricia Cronin: c/o Deitch Projects, 212-941-9475, www.deitch.com

Bettina Werner: www.bettina-werner.com

Silhouettes by **Carol Lebeaux:** 508-842-8730, www.silhouettes-by-carol.com

"Artistic License," art-auction fundraiser for the **Pasadena Humane Society:** 626-792-7151, www.phsspca.org

Art for Animals: www.artforanimals.org

Artist **Daniel Zezelj** published a visually arresting graphic novel called *Stray Dog* while artist-in-residence at Boston's Isabella Stewart Gardner Museum (it includes several images of mutts); for more information, visit www.dzezelj.com.

For more information on the **Shep Memorial** in Fort Benton, MT, go to www.fortbenton.com.

Scented soy candles by Ergo available at **Safe Home Products:** 888-607-9902, www.safehomeproducts.com

Fiesta dog bowls from **Sylvester & Co.:** 631-725-5012

Bauer dog bowls: available at Frank J. Miele Gallery, New York City, 212-876-5775, or www.bauerpottery.com

Colorful steel bowls with slip-proof rubber rings by Prima Pet available at **Fetch:** www.fetchpets.com

The New York Dog: 877-937-6235, www.thenydog.com

Best Friends, publication of Best Friends Animal Society: www.bestfriends.org

Animal Guardian, publication of Doris Day Animal League: www.ddal.org

Animal Watch, publication of ASPCA: www.aspca.org

For a truly dapper large mutt, outfit him for a wedding in a man's wing collar and silk bow tie from A.T. Harris formal wear (212-682-6325, www.atharis.com). Girl dogs prefer to wear the Josie scarf by Elizabeth Gillett (www.elizabethgillett.com) because it sports a silk rose.

Take Your Dog to Work Day is the brainchild of **Pet Sitters International:** 336-983-9222, www.petsit.com.

Totie the border collie mix is a fixture at the Brooklyn, NY, modernist-furniture emporium **The Two Jakes** (www.twojakes.com). She was adopted from **BARC** (www.barcshelter.org) just a few blocks away.

For stores that carry **Doggles,** call 530-344-1635 or visit www.doggles.com.

Aluminum fold-out **ramps** available from www.lambriarvet.com; **Twistep** available from www.twistep.com, 888-284-7742

Flotation vest for canines available from Hamilton Marine: 800-639-2715, www.hamiltonmarine.com; MaiTai, pictured on page 219 modeling the vest, was adopted from the **Humane Society of Boulder Valley in Colorado,** 303-442-4030, www.boulderhumane.org.

Joyride car-seat covers available from Target: www.target.com

Ruff Rider Roadie Canine Vehicle Restraint Training Harness: available at 720-249-2986, www.ruffrider.com

Hydro Bowl travel bowl by Canine Hardware: 800-660-9033, www.caninehardware.com

To order Travel Tummy by **Tasha's Herbs:** 800-315-0142

Ginger Tummy (Traveler Formula): available at www.b-naturals.com

Four Seasons Hotels: www.fourseasons.com

All Animals, publication of the Humane Society of the United States: www.hsus.org

The Bark: 877-227-5639, www.thebark.com

Modern Dog: 866-734-3131, www.moderndog.ca

On the subject of cameras, I've achieved brilliant results with my digital **Leica** camera: 201-767-7500, www.leica-usa.com.

Starwood Hotels and Resorts:
www.starwoodhotels.com

Loews Hotels: www.loewshotels.com

Alexis Hotel, Seattle: www.alexishotel.com

Sherpa: www.sherpapet.net

To book passage for large dogs on an Alitalia freighter jet, call **Mersant International,** 718-978-8200; arrangements must be made at least ten days in advance to allow time for a security background check. For two eighty-pound dogs, the cost is $3,500 each way, plus the price of seats, which sell at normal airfare rates.

Tejas Crates: 972-396-2970, www.tejascrates.com

For information on the **Dog Chapel,** call 800-449-2580 or visit www.huneck.com.

Northwest Airlines: www.nwa.com

Cypress Inn, Carmel: www.cypress-inn.com

Las Ventanas al Paraiso: www.lasventanas.com

Europeds: 415-388-2853, www.europeds.com

While hiking with your mutt, strap some key items to his frame in his very own backpack from **Wolf Packs:** 541-482-7669, www.wolfpacks.com.

Mutt Lynch Winery: 707-942-6180, www.muttlynchwinery.com

Online dating services:

> **www.datefetch.com**
>
> **www.PetPeopleFishing.com**
>
> **www.SinglesWithPets.com**
>
> **www.DateMyPet.com**
>
> **www.SingleDogOwners.com**
>
> **www.LoveMeLoveMyPets.com**
>
> **www.LeashesandLovers.com**

In Cathy Guisewite's comic strip *Cathy*, Cathy and Irving include their two mutts, Electra and Vivian, in their wedding as ring-bearers and register on www.thebigday.com to benefit Pet Orphans of Southern California, a Van Nuys shelter where Guisewite and her daughter volunteer (818-901-0190, www.petorphansfund.org).

THE AUTHOR WOULD LIKE TO EXTEND A MILLION THANKS TO:

Violetta Acocella, Alessandra Alessi, Kevin Bacon and Kyra Sedgwick, Charlotte Barnard, Martha Barnette, Lynda Barry, John Bartlett, Kathy Bauch, Robin Bell, William Berloni, Dr. Rebecca Campbell of Symphony Vet Center, Donna Cerutti, Walter Chin, Lynda Clark, Kathie Coblentz, Deb Davis of Paws With a Cause, Frank DeCaro, Marcello Forte of Animal Haven, Elana Frankel, Dan Tashman, and Cassidy, David Frei, Danny Gregory, Kitty Hawks, Jane Hoffman of the Mayor's Alliance for NYC's Animals, Randi Hoffman and Tara Schapers of Bide-A-Wee, John Huba, Nathaniel Kilcer, Linda Lambert, the Lansbury Family (Emily, George, Elizabeth, Natalie, and Sydney), the other Lansbury Family (Ally Sheedy, Rebecca, and David), Carol Lebeaux, Leica Camera USA, Meredith Lue, John Maher, Marisa Marchetto, Mary Ellen Mark, Patrick McDonnell, Nellie McKay, Chas Miller, Isaac Mizrahi, Eleanor Mondale, Linda Nardi, Sue Nastasi, Todd Oldham, Mackenzie Dawson Parks, Rebecca Paul, Dr. Heather Peikes of Animal Allergy and Dermatology Specialists, Elizabeth Peyton, Melissa Holbrook Pierson and Nelly, Paige Powell, Susan Richmond and Dr. Elizabeth Higgins of the Humane Society of New York, Robert Risko, Kenny Scharf, Scott Shields, Tomoko Shimura, Nancy Soriano, Eric Stoltz, George and Martha Szabo, Estella Warren, Cherylyn Washington of the ASPCA, Bruce Weber, Jennifer Weinik, Linda Wells, Bettina Werner, Dirk Westphal, Lee Wheeler of Hearts United for Animals, Bunny Williams, and Barbara Williamson of Best Friends Animal Society ...

... and Susan Bolotin, Jennifer Griffin, Micah Hales, Lisa Hollander, Denise Sommer, Suzanne Rafer, Leora Kahn, Aaron Clendening, Kristy Ramsammy, Barbara Peragine, Nicki Clendening, Irene Demchyshyn, Katherine Camargo, Wayne Kirn, Melissa Camero, and Katie Workman of Workman Publishing, with a special thank you to Peter Workman for initiating the brilliant concept of a book celebrating the underdog.

thank you

CREDITS

All mutt photography by Jeanette Beckman except the following:

Dedication: p. ii drawing by Robert Risko, originally published in *The New Yorker*

Table of Contents: p. iv Julia Szabo; p. v Mary Ellen Mark (top), drawing by Danny Gregory (bottom)

Foreword: p. vi Julia Szabo

Carrying a Torch for Tiki.: p. viii drawing by Martha Szabo, p. x drawing by Danny Gregory

Welcome to the Tribe: p. 3 Jerry Schulman/Superstock (Black Lab), Dietrich Gehring (Shih Tzu); p. 4 Pat Doyle; p. 6 Photofest (Lucille Ball, Dr. Phil, Julia Roberts), AP Wide World (JFK, Lyndon Johnson); p. 7 AP Wide World (David Duchovny & Téa Leoni, Matthew Broderick & Sarah Jessica Parker, k.d. lang, Harvey Fierstein, Phoebe Cates & Kevin Kline), Photofest (Paul McCartney, Elton John, Ellen DeGeneres, Christian Bale), Jeff Vespa/Wire Image (Hillary Swank), Rick Mackler-Rangefinders/Globe Photos (Paul Auster), Globe Photos (Mark Doty), Christopher Ameruoso, from the book *Pets and Their Stars 2005,* www.chrisaphoto.com (Anthony Kiedis and Muddy), Pat Doyle (Pupwardly Mobile dog); p. 9 Tim Aylen (top); p. 10 AP Wide World (AKC), Anders Blomqvist/Lonely Planet Images (Sweden), David Tipling/Lonely Planet Images (Norway), Emma Miller/Lonely Planet Images (Hungary), Steve Simonsen/Lonely Planet Images (Puerto Rico), Manfred Gottschalk/Lonely Planet Images (England), Jon Davison/Lonely Planet Images (Italy), Chris Mellor/Lonely Planet Images (Japan), Julia Szabo (Puerto Rico dog); p. 13 AP Wide World (JFK Jr., Al Gore, John Kerry), Chad Blackburn (Marsha Blackburn), Photofest

(Jon Stewart), drawings by Danny Gregory; p. 14 AP Wide World/NASA; p. 15 AP Wide World; p. 17 Julia Szabo

Where the Mutts Are: p. 21 Photo Researchers (top), Julia Szabo (bottom); p. 23 paintings by Martha Szabo; p. 25 AP Wild World (top), Dirk Westphal (bottom two); p. 26 Kathleen Moore; p. 30 comic strip by Lynda Barry; p. 32 Superstock (right); p. 36 Neuter/Spay Stamp Design © 2002 United States Postal Service; p. 37 Julia Szabo; p. 39 Ira Fox; p. 40, 41 drawings by Robert Risko, originally published in *The New Yorker;* p. 45 Marcelle Furrow-Kiebler; p. 50 courtesy of Eric Stoltz; p. 52 Todd Oldham; p. 54 Julia Szabo; p. 55 *Life* magazine cover, October 8, 2004. Copyright © 2004 Life Inc. Reprinted with permission. All rights reserved.

Mixology: p. 59 Sue Hartley (top); p. 66 Julia Szabo; p. 67 Brad Kramer; p. 69 Liz Remmel; p. 74 Kenneth McCray/Superstock (Greyhound); p. 75 Ernest Manewall/Superstock (Coyote), Corbis/Punchstock (Collie); p. 76 Tim Davis/Photo Researchers (Rottweiler); p. 77 Tim Davis/Photo Researchers (Rottweiler); p. 78 Jerry Schulman/Superstock (Wheaten), Yann Arthus-Bertrand/Corbis (Cairn, Norwich Terrier); p. 79 Jerry Schulman/Superstock (Wheaten), Yann Arthus-Bertrand/Corbis (Norwich Terrier); p. 81 Punchstock (Boston Terrier), Dietrich Gehring (Shih Tzu); p. 82 Dietrich Gehring (Pit Bull), Carolyn A. Mckeone/Photo Researchers (Pointer), Jerry Schulman/Superstock (Black Lab); p. 84 Superstock (Chow); p. 86 Kenneth McCray/Superstock (Greyhound), Jerry Schulman/Superstock (Black Lab), Corbis/ Punchstock (Collie), Dietrich Gehring (Pit Bull); p. 88 Jerry Schulman/Superstock (Black Lab), Yann Arthus-Bertrand/Corbis (Foxhound); p. 90 Tracy Morgan/Getty Images (Miniature Poodle); p. 91 Tracy Morgan/Getty Images (Miniature Poodle); p. 92 Bob Shirtz/Superstock (Pug); p. 96 Dietrich Gehring (Pit Bull), Carolyn A. McKeone/Photo Researchers (Rhodesian Ridgeback); p. 97 Dietrich Gehring

(Pit Bull); p. 98 Yann Arthus-Bertrand/Corbis (Foxhound), Carolyn A. Mckeone/Photo Researchers (Pointer), Dietrich Gehring (Pit Bull); p. 99 Dietrich Gehring (Pit Bull); p. 100 Dietrich Gehring (Pit Bull); p. 101 Carolyn A. McKeone/Photo Researchers (Beagle, Pointer); p. 102 Superstock (Chow); p. 103 Robert Dowling/Corbis (Briard), Superstock (Chow); p. 104 Courtesy of the Westminster Kennel Club (top), Carolyn A.Mckeone/Photo Researchers (Pointer)

Sound Mutt, Sound Body: p. 116 Julia Szabo; p. 118 Julia Szabo; p. 120 Bob Minenna; 127 Julia Szabo (second dog from right); p. 129 Mary Ellen Mark; p. 132 painting by Martha Szabo; p. 133 drawing by Marisa Marchetto; p. 136 Todd Oldham (bottom), Mellow Mutts (shampoo right), SheaPet (shampoo left); p. 137 Julia Szabo; p. 141 Patrick Rideaux/ Rex USA (Selma Blair); p. 142 silhouette by Carol Lebeaux

Oh, Behave!: p. 145 drawing by Danny Gregory; p. 147 Grove Pashley; p. 149 Pat Doyle; p. 150, 151 Julia Szabo; p. 152 John Currid; p. 157 The Granger Collection; p. 159 drawing by Danny Gregory, photo by Julia Szabo; p. 160 Paige Powell; p. 162 Sue Hartley; p. 163 Julia Szabo (right); p. 165 Julia Szabo; p. 168 Julia Szabo; p. 175 Bruce Weber; p. 176 Julia Szabo; p. 177 Julia Szabo (bottom); p. 178 Bryan Sirotkin (left), courtesy of Paws With a Cause, www.pawswithacause.org (right) p. 179 drawing by Jennifer Weinik; p. 180 drawing by Danny Gregory; p. 181 drawing by Rebecca Lansbury; p. 184 Julia Szabo (top); p. 185 Scott Pasfield (top two)

La Dolce Vita: p. 188 Kathleen Moore (right); p. 190 Julia Szabo (far left, second from right); p. 191 painting by Martha Szabo; p. 193 NYLA (Squeaky Toy), Canine Hardware (Tennis Ball), Kong (Kong toy), Julia Szabo (marrow bone, dental bone); p. 196 Trixie + Peanut; p. 198 dogbooties.com (footwear), Dogz Togz/Bark Slope (sweater); p. 199 Julia Szabo (bottom left), Mary Ellen Mark

(bottom right); p. 201 Grove Pashley; p. 202 Paige Powell; p. 204 NYLA (bottom right); p. 205 Julia Szabo; p. 206 drawing by Marisa Marchetto; p. 207 courtesy of Tyler Hall; p. 210 courtesy of Gavin Brown's Enterprise; p. 211 Jennifer Weinik (left), Patricia Cronin (right); p. 212 Jennifer Weinik; p. 213 Courtesy of Kenny Scharf (top); p. 214 silhouette by Carol Lebeaux; p. 215 Reprinted with permission from *Town & Country*. Photograph by John Huba; p. 217 Susan Goldman; p. 218–219 MINI Cooper/Courtesy of the MINI Division of BMW of North America, LIC; p. 218 Kathleen Moore (bottom); p. 219 Anne Farr Butterfield (top); p. 223 Vallenilla Hector/Gamma; p. 224 Photovault; p. 225 Stephen Huneck Galleries, Inc.; p. 227 Julia Szabo; p. 228 Courtesy of Dogster, www.dogster.com; p. 229 Christopher Ameruoso, from the book *Pets and Their Stars 2005*, www.chrisaphoto.com; p. 230 drawing by Marisa Marchetto, Walter Chin (bottom photo); p. 233 Jeff McNamara

The Ulti-Mutt Resource Guide: p. 235 drawing by Danny Gregory; p. 236 drawing by Danny Gregory; p. 237 Copyright © Patrick McDonnell. Reprinted with permission of King Features Syndicate; p. 239 Copyright © Patrick McDonnell. Reprinted with permission of King Features Syndicate; p. 240 drawing by Danny Gregory; p. 241 courtesy of ASPCA; p. 242 courtesy of Harry Barker; p. 243 drawing by Danny Gregory; p. 244 Julia Szabo (top), drawing by Danny Gregory; p. 245 drawing by Danny Gregory; p. 246 Michael Nastasi, Copyright © Patrick McDonnell. Reprinted with permission of King Features Syndicate; p. 247 drawing by Danny Gregory; p. 248 Julia Szabo (top), drawing by Danny Greory; p. 249 drawing by Danny Gregory; p. 250 Bettina Werner; p. 251 Jonathon Kambouris; p. 252 Copyright © Cathy Guisewite. Reprinted with permission of Universal Press Syndicate.

INDEX